19/97

Date Due

04/06 29			

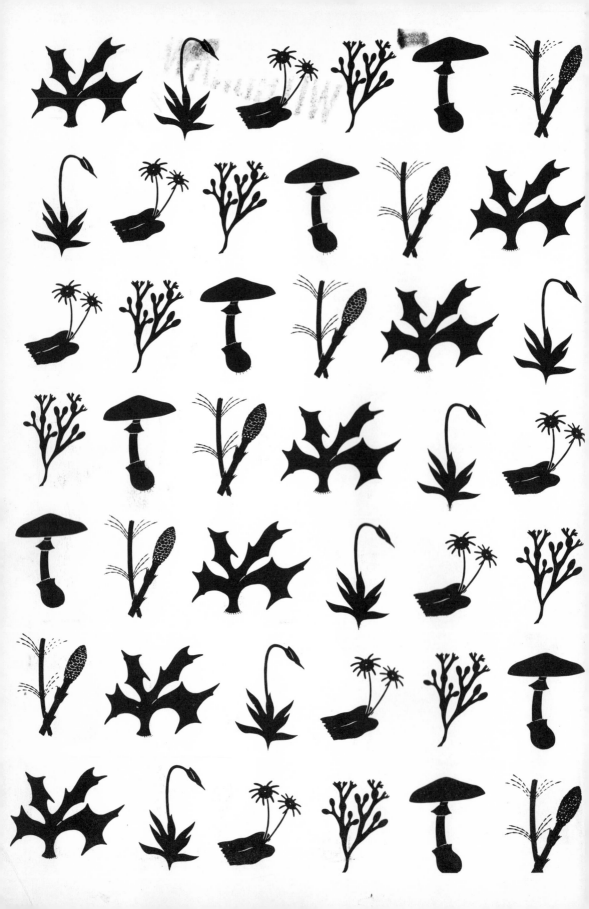

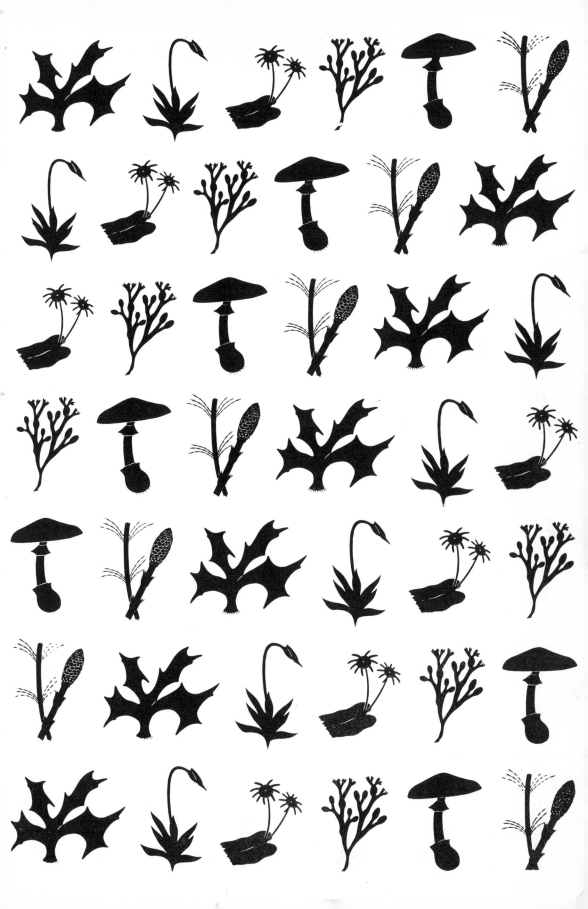

Identification of plants shown on end sheets (see previous page). Top row, left to right: lichen, moss plant, liverwort, alga (*fucus*, a seaweed), mushroom (*Amanita*), horsetail (*Equisetum*).

Plants Without Leaves

Plants Without Leaves

LICHENS   FUNGI   MOSSES   LIVERWORTS
SLIME-MOLDS   ALGAE   HORSETAILS

Ross E. Hutchins

Photographs by the author

DODD, MEAD & COMPANY · NEW YORK

Frontispiece: A Parmelia *lichen, commonly found on tree bark*

All photographs are by the author except those on pages 87 and 89 which are used through the courtesy of Dr. Martin H. Zimmermann, Harvard University.

Introduction

$\mathcal{M}$uch of the earth is clothed with green plants that add beauty to hills and meadows and soften the bleak outlines of rocks and cliffs. Most of these plants are trees, flowers, and grasses, many of which grow to large size. But there are other, less known, little plants that also play their parts in making the world a pleasant place in which to live. These are the liverworts, mosses, horsetails, lichens, and fungi.

Most of these "little plants" inhabit mountain glens or grow in the vicinities of quiet woodland streams. Others live in the sea or in lakes and rivers. The fungi thrive in damp places upon vegetable mold accumulated from the decay of leaves and wood of other years. Some fungi, perhaps the most interesting kinds, grow upon fallen trees. The colorful slime-molds creep slowly over damp, decaying wood and, in time, form strange, spore cases, each on a separate stalk. By contrast, the lichens prefer the sun where they spread their creeping growths over soil, rocks and the trunks of living trees, often at high altitudes where weather is always cold.

While most of these plants are partial to warm or temperate climates, the lichens and mosses thrive far beyond the Arctic Circle. Probably no other forms of plant life have been able to adapt themselves to such wide climatic ranges.

This, then, is the story of the small, leafless plants that form green carpets over forest floors or rocks to cushion the tread of our feet, or add touches of living color to decaying wood or barren landscapes. It is also the story of the algae that form the "pastures of the sea." These plants produce no colorful blooms nor grow to large size, yet among them are found some of the world's most interesting and unusual plants.

—R. E. H.

Contents

Lichens grow upon trees, rocks, or the ground. Each lichen actually consists of two forms of plant life—an alga and a fungus.

CHAPTER 1

Meet the Leafless Plants

The Algae: Most of us have seen algae (pronounced al-jee; singular is alga) of one kind or another. The green, stringy growth often observed in ponds is made up of algal filaments, and algae are abundant in the sea. Other kinds grow as a green "bloom" on the ground, on tree bark, or even upon ice and snow. The largest algae live in the sea and are called seaweeds. Some seaweeds, called kelps, may be more than 150 feet long.

The Fungi: These are simple forms of plant life that have no green coloring matter or chlorophyll, and must thus obtain their food from other living things. Some fungi (pronounced funj-eye; singular is fungus), such as the mushrooms, live on the ground or on rotten wood, obtaining food from organic matter; others are parasitic in or on living plants and animals.

The Slime-molds: These are among the world's strangest plants, and whether they are really plants or animals is still a matter of opinion among biologists. They live in rotten wood where they creep about like great amoebae. Later, they form stalked, spore-bearing structures. Often these are of beautiful and remarkable form.

The Lichens: These little plants are of varied form and coloration and grow upon rocks, soil, or the bark of trees, all the way from the tropics to polar regions. Sometimes they are erroneously

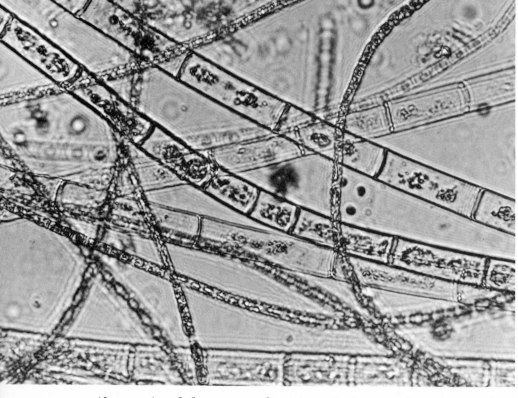

Algae are found almost everywhere, from the Arctic to the Antarctic. They occur in the sea, in fresh water, on trees, and on soil. Shown here are greatly enlarged strands of fresh-water algae.

called mosses. A lichen (pronounced li-ken) actually consists of two plants, an alga and a fungus, so closely associated together that they seem to be one plant.

The Liverworts: If you explore the margins of woodland streams or the vicinities of shady springs you are apt to see green, creeping plants of flat, leaflike form growing over the ground or upon rocks. These are the liverworts, primitive plants that were probably among the first to live upon dry land.

The Mosses: Like other small, leafless plants, the mosses are primitive forms that reproduce by spores instead of seeds. Like liverworts, they prefer damp, shady habitats and the ground in such places is often covered with soft, green carpets of mosses.

The Horsetails: During the ancient Devonian age, about 350 million years ago, there flourished great treelike plants with jointed stems and twiglike "leaves." We are familiar with their small, modern descendants which we call horsetails because of their form of growth.

THE STORY

This is the story of the world's small leafless plants which usually grow in the sea, in fresh water or damp places, upon rocks, or on the bark of trees. While they are of lowly birth and ancient ancestry, among them are found some of the most interesting of all forms of plant life. They are somewhat mysterious in their manners of growth, largely because they reproduce themselves

Fungi are simple forms of plant life having no green chlorophyll. They cannot manufacture their own food and must live on food obtained from other plants and from animals. The tiny mushrooms here grew upon tree bark.

Are slime-molds plants or animals? In the sporangia stage they are like plants. This is a cluster of red Arcyria *sporangia growing on a piece of rotten wood. Millions of spores are contained in the spongelike fibers.*

by microscopic spores, rather than by seeds. Such common plants as violets and sunflowers we can easily understand; they grow from seeds planted in the ground and we are familiar with their growth habits. Unfortunately, most of us know far less about the world's small, non-flowering plants.

People are usually interested in things of record size: the biggest tree, the largest fish, or the largest flowers. But "littleness" is also of interest. Observing small plants through a microscope or hand lens can be a most fascinating and revealing experience. The nature photographer is continually viewing small living things through the lenses of his cameras and seeing the wonders they reveal. One may walk through a forest and admire the tall trees, but when one peers through a lens at a moss or a lichen he is seeing a miniature world that he can never actually enter. He is always an outsider and his size prevents his ever actually taking

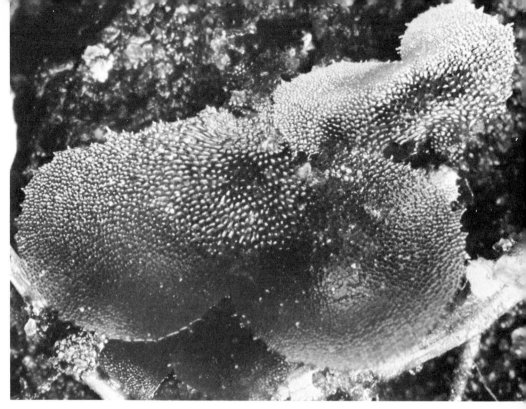

Green liverworts creep over damp earth or stones in shady places. They are lowly forms of plant life, with no true leaves, stems, or roots. They reproduce by spores instead of seeds.

part in the tiny dramas enacted there. He may see an ant crawling through a green, mossy jungle, but the ant lives in a different realm that is, seemingly, governed by different physical laws. If a woodland deer should tumble over a precipice it would be killed, but an ant may fall from the limb of a tree and alight upon a mossy bank unharmed. Size is what makes the difference. A tree needs space and large amounts of water to survive, but a bit of moss or liverwort can thrive on a trickle of moisture from a woodland spring. Each type of plant—the largest and the smallest—is fitted to the life it leads.

The plants without leaves grow almost everywhere, from the tropics to the cold lands beyond the Arctic and Antarctic Circles. Lichens, especially, thrive where least expected, even on desert rocks. Mosses, liverworts, and fungi prefer moist habitats, usually being found in shady situations along brooks and streams. Fungi grow almost any place where there is sufficient moisture, especially in warmer climates.

If we travel northward, we come eventually to the edge of the "tree line" near the Arctic Circle. South of this line stretches the unbroken forest, but beyond this point grow only the little plants that hug the ground seeking shelter from cold Arctic blasts. We have the same experience when we climb a high mountain. Up beyond the forests that clothe the lower slopes is a realm where only mosses, lichens and a few brave flowering plants grow hidden among the rocks. Tall plants cannot survive the cold and the wind.

The leafless plants are always the first to grow where natural catastrophes have occurred. They heal the wounds caused by landslides and avalanches and the cutting away of banks by streams. The jagged surfaces of rocks torn apart by earthquakes are soon covered by creeping lichens. They slowly cover the scars

This bit of earth is covered with moss plants. Mosses also grow on bark and stones. They appear to have green leaves, but these are not true leaves. Millions of years ago, some mosses grew to large size.

Imagine that this is a forest of giant, treelike horsetails a hundred feet tall. That is probably how the horsetail or Equisetum *forests looked during the Devonian period. These modern shoots grow only a foot or two high.*

made by earth's greatest forces. To bare expanses of cliffs and, sometimes, even to city pavements, mosses add touches of restful green that break the dreary monotony.

Woods, on a sunny day in summer, are pleasant and colorful. The leaves are green and form shifting patterns of light and shadow upon the forest floor. But when the sun is gone and soft rains fall, the leaves are no longer bright green and the once-colorful flowers droop on their stems. It is then that the mosses, liverworts, and lichens come into their own. They absorb the falling rain and take on their brightest hues. Lichens that, during

17

dry weather, look like patches of gray paint on the trunks of trees, absorb moisture and dress themselves in bright shades of green and gold. Thus does Nature balance her books; the bright colors of leaves and flowers in the sunlight are replaced by the attractive hues of the little, creeping plants in the rain.

Most of us are fair-weather people; we abhor the rain and seek shelter when it comes. But we miss seeing the woods at a time when they take on one of their most attractive personalities. A walk in rainy woods has its compensations. Not only are the colors of mosses and lichens more brilliant, but upon each moss-head glows a droplet of water, sparkling like a jewel. When the rain clouds are gone and the sun comes out again these droplets shine even more brilliantly for a time until they evaporate away into the air. Under hot sun, the mosses and lichens lose their moisture and dry up, awaiting the coming of another shower when they will "bloom" again. It is during showers, too, that small, creeping things—the snails and slugs—come out of their hidden retreats and crawl over the damp carpets of mosses and liverworts, leaving shining trails behind. They, like the little plants among which they live, are not lovers of the hot sunshine. After the rains are gone, the fungi—the mushrooms and toadstools—push up out of the ground, stimulated to growth by the water that has seeped below the surface.

Thus, the woods and forests are different places when the leaves are wet with rain and when the ground is damp with early-morning dew and the webs of spiders glisten like strings of jewels in the morning sun. Summer showers and morning dew— these are what the little creeping plants like best.

THE CURTAIN RISES

Time and plant life are closely tied together. There was a time many millions of years ago when the only land plants were mosses, liverworts, and ferns. Probably there were also fungi. All these plants reproduced themselves by means of spores instead

Lichens are common on the trunks of trees. Here a tree frog rests on tree bark among lichens. Its body is marked to resemble the lichen-covered bark.

of seeds. But the world spun on through space and the eons slowly passed. At first the climate of the world was warm and tropical and very favorable to plant growth; then the climates began to change. Sometimes they turned cool for millions of years; then they were warm again. These changes, perhaps, stimulated the creation of plants of new types, better suited to climatic variations. Eventually, the flowering plants appeared upon the stage. These plants reproduced by seeds and soon covered all the habitable parts of the globe. But, strangely, the old-fashioned, spore-producing plants continued on down through time,

19

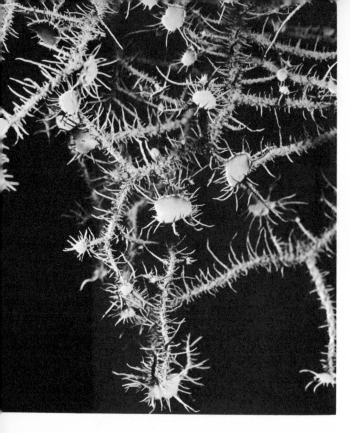

Some lichens grow suspended from tree branches as does this one known as old-man's-beard lichen (Usnea).

but little changed except for the fact that most of them gradually became smaller in size. The liverworts have changed hardly at all.

Just how these ancient plants have survived as the world has changed is something of a mystery. Probably it is because they can live where other plants cannot. Mosses and lichens can eke out life upon barren rock or cold, stony soil where no flowering plant could exist. This is no doubt the secret of their survival in the modern world where plants are continually in direct competition with each other for places in the sun. No plant can continue to exist in nature if it is not just a little better adapted to the place it lives than some other plant. If a plant cannot adapt, it soon becomes extinct. The same is true of animals. The world's sedimentary stratas are strewn with the fossils of both plants and animals that became extinct because they could not withstand the competition. That is the law of Nature. She is a hard taskmaster that plays no favorites.

CHAPTER 2

Algae: The First Plants

The algae are simple forms of plant life found growing in the sea, in fresh water, and on land. Their ancestors, living in the sea, were probably the first plants. With the formation of streams and lakes the algae (singular: alga) became adapted to life in fresh or non-salty water. At present they occur almost everywhere. About 4,000 kinds have been found north of the Arctic Circle and they are also abundant in Antarctic regions. Algae of some kinds have taken up life on land but the sea is their ancestral home and it is there that they have reached their greatest diversity in both form and number.

Most of us are familiar with the threadlike or filamentous algae such as *Spirogyra* found in lakes and streams where they form green, stringy masses in the water. If we dwell in cities we have certainly seen the result of algal growth in swimming pools. This is the greenish, slimy growth which must be controlled by means of chemicals. Algae also grow as a green "bloom" on the sides of trees and fence posts, especially in damp situations. Sometimes this algal growth is confined to the north or shady sides of trees and thus is used as an indicator of direction by which persons lost in the woods may sometimes find their way. Algae of other kinds seem able to grow at low temperatures and so are found growing on snow or on the faces of glaciers. Most interesting of all, probably, are those remarkable algae that thrive in the waters

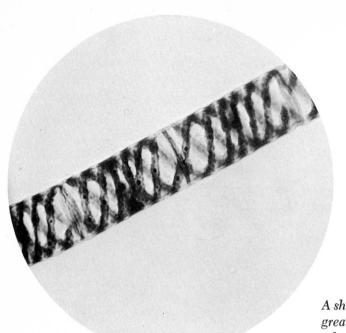

A short section of Spirogyra greatly magnified. The spiral strands are chloroplasts which contain green chlorophyll by which the plant manufactures food.

These highly magnified strands of Zygnema, a common alga, show how conjugation or fertilization occurs between adjacent strands. New algal filaments arise as a result of this fertilization.

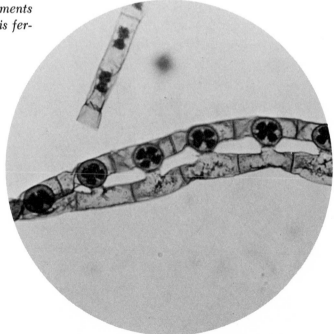

Valonia algae are the world's largest cells. Each one is a single cell, even though it may be two or three inches in diameter. Because of their large size, these algal cells are used in research in osmosis and related studies of cellular physiology. Found in the sea, they are known as "sea bottles."

of hot springs. The best place to observe these latter algae is in Yellowstone National Park. Anyone who has visited this area has noticed the bright coloration in the hot springs and pools. These colors range from bright orange to blue and result from the growth of algae which are adapted to life in water not far below the boiling point. These are the so-called blue-green algae (*Cyanophyta*) that occur also in soil, on the sides of damp stones or on clay pots in greenhouses. Those kinds that live in hot springs can grow in water at temperatures as high as 185°F., which is far too hot for the hand to bear. The specimens pictured here were obtained from Yellowstone National Park by swiftly plucking the growth from the water. My hand could stand immersion in the hot water for only a second or so. It is quite amazing that these lowly forms of plant life can live and grow at such temperatures. These thermal algae have the ability to precipitate

The waters of geysers and hot springs of Yellowstone National Park are, in many cases, near the boiling point. Yet many kinds of colored algae live in these waters at temperatures as high as 185° F.

the calcium and magnesium salts out of the hot, mineralized water and to deposit it in the form of a hard mineral called *travertine*. The result is that travertine deposits are found in and around almost all of the hot springs and geysers. Most of the color in the hot springs of Yellowstone Park is the direct result of living, algal growth.

One often hears of "red snow" and some people, especially in the past, have believed that it had some supernatural origin. Actually, "red snow" is the result of the abundant growth of a red alga called *Chlorophyta* which contains a red pigment known as *haematochrome*. Green chlorophyll is also present in the alga but it is masked by the abundant red pigment so that the plants appear to be red. Strange, indeed, is the fact that this "red snow" alga is rather closely related to the algae which live in hot springs. Red algae also live in sea water. For instance, the Red Sea received its name from the red algae that color its waters.

In the world there are about 1,400 kinds of blue-green algae, most of which live in fresh water. The "pea soup" appearance of still ponds also results from the abundant growth of these algae. One alga of this type is *Nostoc*, often found growing in ponds and quiet pools where it forms jelly-like balls almost an inch in diameter. This alga, when dried, may remain alive for a long while. For example, it was found that such dried *Nostoc* would revive and grow after having been dried for eighty-seven years.

While most of the common pond-living algae are of simple form—that is, they are single-celled or grow in threadlike strings —there are many kinds of marine algae that grow to large size and have definite forms like land plants. Examples are seaweeds such as *Sargassum* weed, sea-lettuce (*Ulva*), devil's apron (*Laminaria*), kelp (*Nereocystis*) and numerous other kinds. While these plants are called seaweeds, they are all algae of primitive types that never left the sea. Such marine algae often reach large size and have rootlike attachments called *holdfasts* to anchor them to

This photomicrograph shows blue-green algae from a hot spring in Yellowstone National Park. It was collected from water at 175° F.

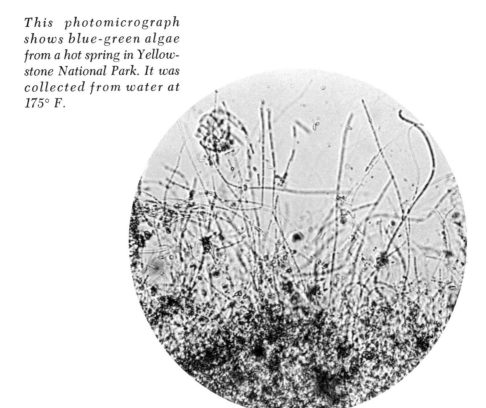

the bottom, but they differ greatly from land plants. Plants, in order to live on land, must have a number of special adaptations. They must have water-conducting or *vascular* systems to carry water and food materials up from the roots, and they must also have strong or woody stems to hold them erect. In other words, there must be a high specialization of parts. By contrast, plants such as algae that live beneath the surface of the sea, need no water-conducting system, no true roots to absorb water, and no woody structures in their stems. Even though a large marine alga, such as bull kelp, may grow 150 feet long, it simply floats in the sea and absorbs its water and minerals through its surface. Sea water, which contains all the minerals needed for growth, furnishes all the raw materials that the plant needs.

On the other hand, a large plant living in the sea must have certain specializations. In order to remain near the surface where it can obtain sufficient sunlight, it must be prevented from sinking too deep. When sunlight falls upon water a large part of it is reflected from the surface and is thus lost to submerged plants. Sunlight is made of rays of different wavelengths and these rays do not all penetrate water to the same depth. Only 2 per cent of the red light rays penetrate to six feet. On the other hand, about 75 per cent of the blue rays reach this depth. As depths increase, the amount of light decreases very rapidly until, at 300 feet, there are no red rays at all. Beyond 300 feet, only blue and indigo rays are present. Since blue rays are readily absorbed by water, deep seas are blue in color. Returning now to the marine algae which must depend upon green chlorophyll to manufacture their food, it is a fact that chlorophyll needs much red light. Thus, green plants, such as algae, cannot live at great depths because they do not get the proper kind of light there. Since they require large amounts of red light they must remain near the surface.

Large algae such as kelps and *Sargassum* weeds are prevented from sinking by means of gas-filled floats or bladders which func-

Bladder kelp, or Nereocystis, *is a large alga that grows in the sea. Its "roots" are attached to the bottom, while the air-filled bladder holds the fronds up near the surface where they receive light.*

tion in the same way as do glass or cork floats in supporting fish nets. Also, since these algae may live in water as deep as 75 feet, they must have some means of attachment to prevent their drifting onto the shore. This is why they are anchored to the bottom by holdfasts. While holdfasts of marine algae may resemble the roots of land-inhabiting plants, they are not really roots at all and play no part in obtaining minerals and water for the plant.

While the marine algae have never become as diversified in form as the land plants, among them are found many kinds of varied and interesting types. One of these is the sea palm (*Pos-*

telsia palmaeformis) which grows about a foot tall and resembles a small palm tree. Another pretty sea alga is the sea-mushroom (*Acetabularia*) which looks like a tiny, delicate mushroom. There are many other attractive kinds. Sea-lettuce, found growing in many quiet estuaries, resembles nothing so much as delicate leaves of lettuce waving gracefully back and forth with the movements of the currents. *Sargassum* weed, also called gulf weed, has leaflike blades and, scattered about over its surface, are the small air bladders mentioned above. This weed grows in great masses on the Sargasso Sea which lies east of Florida and the West Indies and extends from the Bahamas to the Azores.

The Sargasso Sea gets its name from a Portuguese word, *sargasso*, meaning "grape." This refers to the grapelike clusters of air floats found on the plants growing there. The Sargasso Sea is a vast area, nearly as large as the United States. Actually, it is not really a sea nor is it surrounded by land. It is a portion of the

These daisy-like algae, Acetabularia, *live in the sea where they grow attached to rocks or other submerged objects. About an inch tall, they are often called "sea mushrooms" or "mermaids' parasols."*

Sargassum *weed is an alga that floats in the sea. The Sargasso Sea is covered by this weed. This portion of* Sargassum *weed shows the "leaves" and
the air-filled bladders which keep it afloat.*

Atlantic Ocean, more or less oval in form and covering an area
about 1,000 miles by 2,000 miles or nearly two million square
miles. Since the waters of the Atlantic Ocean are caused to ro-
tate in a clockwise direction by the rotation of the earth and the
contours of the surrounding continents, the Sargasso Sea is like a
great, slowly spinning whirlpool. In this great whirlpool, *Sargassum* weed has been growing for perhaps millions of years. The
first people to see this strange sea were Christopher Columbus
and his men who passed through it in 1492. The men were terri-

fied since they feared that their fragile sailing ships would be trapped in the entangling weed which completely covered the surface of the sea in great floating mats. Since that time, various superstitions have grown up among seafaring men concerning this strange sea of weed. It was believed, for example, that the Sargasso Sea was a "graveyard of ships," that wrecked sailing vessels often floated into this sea to be trapped forever in the great, rotating mass of weed. We now know, of course, that this is not so.

The Sargasso Sea has been in existence since prehistoric times, and constitutes an abundant source of food for sea creatures; thus it is not surprising that a large number of living animals have become adapted to life there. This weedy sea literally teems with unusual fishes, crabs, sea slugs, and other creatures. Since these creatures have been living there for so long they have become remarkably adapted or fitted to life there. Many of them have strange shapes and appendages which serve to camouflage them among the brown strands of seaweed. One of the strangest of these animals is the Sargassum fish (*Pterophryne*) whose body is colored to mimic the weeds among which it lives. In addition to coloration, its fins and other parts are of strange form, making it difficult to see as it rests among the strands of *Sargassum*. Here then, is the world's strangest sea, an area where sea animals of many kinds have taken up their abodes and where they live in fierce competition with each other.

The kelps, mentioned previously, are golden-brown in color and have smooth leathery stalks. They vary in length from a few feet to more than a hundred. These and some other marine algae have considerable economic importance since they are good sources of potassium, iodine and other substances. These algae have the ability of being able to extract and concentrate many chemical elements from sea water. As high as 35 per cent of dry kelp may be potassium chloride and there is nearly 20,000 times as much iodine in kelp as in the sea water in which it lives.

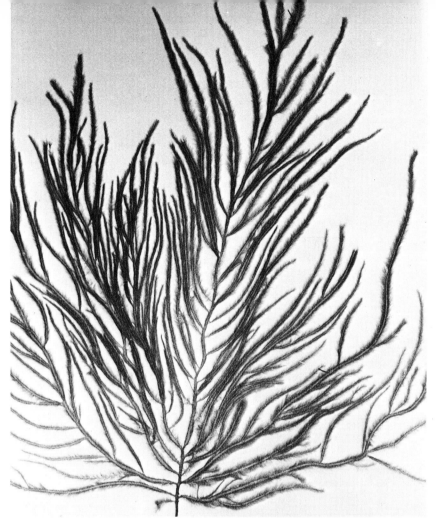

Dasya *is a red alga of the sea. Its delicate branches are feather-like. It is found in tidal waters and has a beautiful red pigmentation.*

Farmers, living along the coasts of northern Europe, formerly collected kelp and used it to fertilize their fields, and seaweeds were also, at one time, fed to cattle and sometimes used as human food. Here in our own country seaweed is often eaten as a "health food." There is good reason for this since sea algae, in addition to containing most of the mineral elements needed for growth, are also good sources of various vitamins, including vitamins A, B-12, C, and D, as well as thiamin, riboflavin, niacin, and pantothenic acid.

From a red seaweed known as Irish moss, or *carrageen*, an

excellent dessert was made in former years. Dulse, another sea-weed, was used as a thickener for soups. Agar, obtained from red seaweed, is used in making bacterial culture media as well as in canning fish and meat. It also finds use in the manufacture of sherbets, ices, candy and bakery products. *Algin*, obtained from brown kelp, is a similar product and is used in the making of antacid tablets, calamine lotion, laxatives and other medicines. It is also used in the manufacture of cosmetics, rubber, textile products, decal adhesives, and glues, and in the making of paints, leather finishes, and sugar.

Seaweed used in the above products is harvested along the coast of Brittany by means of boats. A long tool with a sickle-like end is used to cut the weed, which is then twirled as one winds spaghetti around a fork, and hauled aboard. After drying on a grassy field it is crammed into sacks. Five tons of weed, when dry, weigh only one ton and when this is processed at the factory produces only 200 pounds of alga powder.

The price of seaweeds used in commerce varies considerably. Some kinds sell for as much as $350 per ton, while agar obtained from seaweed sells for from $3.50 to $4.00 per pound. In 1960, the value of seaweed harvested from the waters surrounding the United States amounted to more than two million dollars and its use is expected to increase.

At present, algae of various kinds, especially fresh-water types, are being investigated as a means of feeding spacemen on long, interplanetary flights. It is believed that algae, grown in tanks, may supply much of the food needed during such journeys. Certain algae, when fermented, produce methane and other gases which may be converted into such fuels as gasoline and kerosene.

Algae have also been responsible for the formation of geological deposits. The deposit of travertine by the algae that live in hot springs has already been mentioned. Algae of many other kinds are able to extract calcium from water and deposit it in the form of lime or calcium carbonate either in their cell walls or in

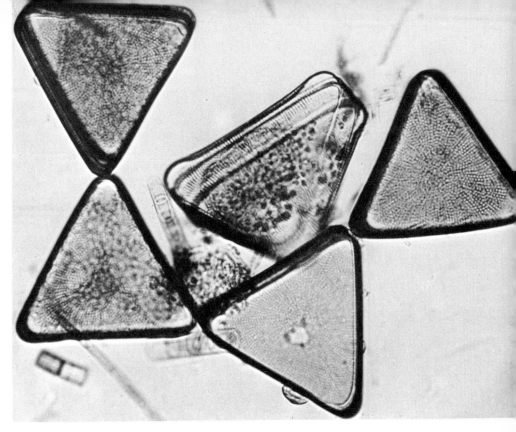

These are diatoms, a form of algae common in water. Each one is an individual cell contained in a glasslike box of silica having a top and a lid. The one at the center, turned slightly on edge, shows the way the lid fits over the box. These algae may truly be said to live in glass houses.

gelatinous sheaths. Over long periods of time such algae have been responsible for the building up of large deposits of limestone and in this way they have played an important role, along with coral animals, in the formation of coral reefs and islands. Blue-green algae that once lived in cool shallow waters deposited layered crusts of limestone which, in some places, may be 1,000 feet thick. *Diatoms*, which are simple forms of algae, have cell walls composed of glasslike silica. There are about 16,000 different kinds of diatoms, many of which are of beautiful and interesting geometric shapes. Most diatoms are found in the sea and when these microscopic plants die, their remains settle to the bottom where thick deposits of *diatomaceous earth* are slowly built up. Some of these deposits, such as those found in Cali-

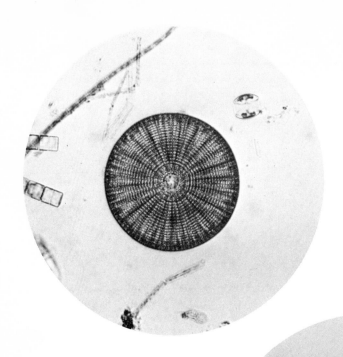

Minute objects of great beauty, diatoms have been called "jewels of the sea." This one, Cyclotella, *is common in ponds. It is magnified about 600 times natural size.*

The diatom Tabellaria *is usually found in groups or chains attached together at alternate corners.*

fornia, are 1,400 feet thick. Diatomaceous earth is used in industry as a filtering agent for gasoline, sugar and other things during processing. It is also used as an insulating material around steam pipes, and as a polishing or scouring agent. Due to its absorbent nature, it is used to absorb and hold liquid nitroglycerin in the making of dynamite.

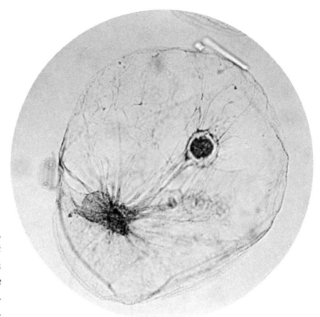

Noctiluca is a microscopic, single-celled animal that lives in warm seas. When disturbed, it emits flashes of greenish light. Some microscopic algae have a similar characteristic.

Of special interest is a group of algae known as the *dinoflagellates*. These are chiefly marine and their cell walls consist of polygonal plates of cellulose. Some kinds emit light, and anyone who has cruised at night in tropical seas has seen these algae, perhaps without knowing what they were. Almost everywhere in the warmer seas one sees their phosphorescence in the water at night. This is in the form of bright "sparks" of light that appear along the sides of ships as the water is disturbed. These tiny flashes can also be seen near beaches if the hand is moved rapidly through the water. The flashes of light are something like the flashing of fireflies. A protozoon, or single-celled animal called *Noctiluca* is also common in warm seas and also gives off sparks of light.

Marine algae constitute the main bulk of the floating plant and animal life of the sea which we call *plankton*, the "sea food" that is fed upon by whales and many lesser creatures that make the oceans of the world their home. It is believed by some scientists that these "sea pastures" may someday furnish a large part of our own food.

This is the "destroying angel" (Amanita phalloides), one of the most deadly of all mushrooms, but one often confused with edible kinds. It is identified by its cuplike base and the collar or veil around the stem just beneath the cap (not visible in this view).

CHAPTER 3

Fungi: Believe-It-or-Not Plants

Of all the world's plants the fungi (singular: fungus) are probably the most mysterious. Fungus molds appear on bread and other foods as if by magic, and mushrooms and toadstools seem to spring up mysteriously on lawns overnight. Other fungi grow on rotten wood or other such places. Some kinds live in or on plants or animals as parasites; some fungi shine in the dark. Luminous fungi growing on rotten wood cause "fox fire."

The study of fungi is called *mycology* and scientists who specialize in their study are called *mycologists.* Fungi are the most numerous of all living things; in the world there are about 250,000 kinds and they range in size from microscopic forms to mushrooms several feet in diameter. A huge mushroom was once found at Walacha, Australia, which weighed over seventeen pounds and measured five feet, two inches in circumference.

Regarding the ancestral origin of fungi, we have very little information. Of course, mycologists have a number of theories. Certainly, fungi are very simple forms of plant life but just what their relationships to other plants are is uncertain. The ancient mosses, ferns and other plants left fossilized remains, but the fungi, being soft and fleshy, left no such clues to their origins, which adds another bit of mystery to them.

Fungi, unlike most other plants, do not contain green chlorophyll and so cannot manufacture their own food. For this reason

Here we see Xylaria *fungi growing on an old magnolia seed cone. These fungi are also common on decaying wood.*

they must obtain their nourishment from other forms of life, either plant or animal. Most fungi live upon dead organic matter such as that found in the soil or in decaying wood. Other fungi have taken up evil habits and become parasitic on plants and animals. Some of our most serious and destructive plant diseases are caused by fungi. The great Irish famine of 1845 to 1860 was caused by late blight of potatoes, a fungus disease which destroyed crops, causing a million people to die of starvation. During this time, another million and a half people were forced to emigrate to other countries, including the United States. The Irish people had become so dependent upon potatoes that the loss of this crop brought about widespread starvation.

Almost every wild and cultivated plant has one or more fungus diseases. Some of these plant-infecting fungi require more than one host plant for the completion of their life histories. For instance, cedar-apple rust forms large galls on cedar trees. These galls produce large numbers of fungus spores which are carried by winds to apple trees where a rust disease is caused. Another example is wheat rust which passes from wheat to barberry and back to wheat again. There are also a number of serious animal and human diseases caused by fungi; the most common of these is athlete's foot, a fungus infection of the skin.

As if to balance the book, many fungi are useful to us both as sources of food and of important drugs. Penicillin, for example, is produced by *Penicillium* fungus or mold. Other "wonder drugs" are obtained from fungi of other kinds. Gibberellin, a substance obtained from a fungus *(Gibberella fujikuroi)*, is a powerful plant growth stimulant. The fungus itself causes a disease of rice.

Probably the most remarkable and interesting of all beneficial fungi are those that live in the soil and trap nematodes, or microscopic worms, that injure the roots of growing plants.

This photomicrograph of Penicillium *shows the fungus in its spore-producing stage. The dark spheres are* conidia *spores which break off and start new growths. The drug penicillin is obtained from this common fungus.*

These strange little fungi, Patella, *grow on rotting wood. They are bright orange in color and are one-eighth inch in diameter.*

Many strange fungi grow on fallen trees and logs that are rotting. This is Poria *which grows flat against the wood. It is related to the bracket fungi that grow like little shelves on the sides of trees.*

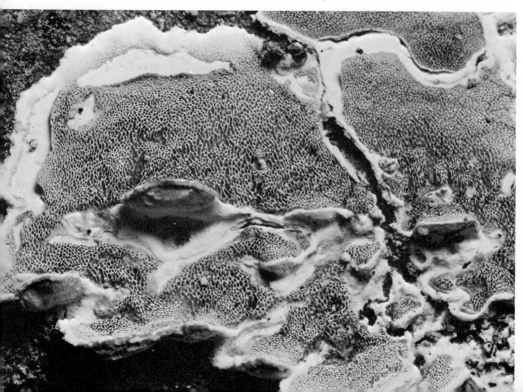

Insects are often destroyed by fungi. This cricket was killed by a fungus which grew inside its body and then produced spore-bearing shoots on the outside.

There are several different kinds of the nematode-trapping fungi and they use different methods to trap or catch their game. One kind, named *Dactylella*, has adhesive or sticky knobs that capture nematodes. Once trapped, the nematode is consumed by the fungus. Someone has called the sticky knobs "lethal lollipops," certainly a very appropriate name. Other fungi, such as *Dactylaria*, use a snare or lasso type of trap. Along the threadlike strands of this latter fungus are located small loops or rings. If a nematode, crawling through the soil, tries to pass through one of these loops it is trapped and the fungus strands then grow into its body to absorb nourishment. Few people are aware of these strange soil-inhabiting fungi, yet they are quite common.

Yeasts, also classified as fungi, are of importance to man. While some yeasts are harmful, others cause the fermentation of sugar, resulting in the production of carbon dioxide gas and alcohol. Baker's yeast, of course, causes bread to rise by its production of gas. The flavors of various kinds of cheeses result from special kinds of molds.

41

This is one of the most beautiful of all mushrooms. It is known as Caesar's mushroom, or royal agaric (Amanita caesarea). Although a close relative of the deadly Amanitas, it is not poisonous. It should not be eaten, however, since it may be easily confused with the deadly kinds. Its cap is bright red or orange while its gills are yellow.

Parasol mushrooms (Lepiota) are common on lawns and in woods. They are edible, but may easily be confused with the highly poisonous Amanitas.

Danger, poisonous! This is the fly agaric (Amanita muscaria). *Note its swollen base and the veil or* annulus *around the stem. People have often died from eating these mushrooms.*

While a few mushrooms, sometimes called toadstools, are poisonous, many may be edible. Probably the most poisonous mushrooms are the *Amanitas*, of which there are at least two very poisonous kinds. One of these is the fly agaric, an *Amanita* which has a bright red or orange cap, and the destroying angel or deadly *Amanita* which has a white cap decorated with scattered, warty patches. These, of course, are not the only poisonous mushrooms and any mushroom found in the woods should be eaten only after definite and positive identification. The common edible mushroom (*Agaricus campestris*) can be bought in a

Growing on a fallen tree, this attractive Polyporus fungus looks like a funnel on a stem. This specimen was solitary, but they often grow in clusters on stumps or logs.

The fungus Sparassis looks something like a cabbage. It grows on the ground and some specimens may be two feet in diameter. Their color varies from white to pale yellow. They belong to the coral fungus family.

This large pore mushroom (Boletus) *is very pretty. The top of the cap is orange, while the underside and stem are yellow. Instead of radiating gills, the undersurfaces have pores within which spores are produced.*

grocery store but it also grows wild almost everywhere. Commercially, mushrooms are usually grown in caves, dark cellars, abandoned mines, or in specially built mushroom cellars where both humidity and temperature are carefully controlled. Beds are "planted" with mushroom "spawn" consisting of threadlike *mycelia* (singular: *mycelium*).

There are many kinds of mushrooms and their study and identification can be an interesting hobby. Many are very beautiful; some are bright scarlet while others are blue, purple, or other gay colors. If the cap of a freshly collected mushroom is placed upon a sheet of paper and covered with a bowl it will be found, after a few hours, that a pretty, radiating pattern appears upon the paper beneath the cap. This is caused by the microscopic spores falling from the gills. These spores are of various colors, depending on the kind of mushroom. They range from white to brown, green, pink, or yellow and are important clues to the identification of the mushrooms. The poisonous *Amanita* mushrooms, for example, have white spores.

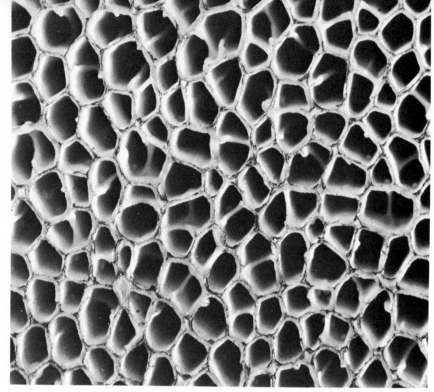

This close-up shows the pores on the undersurface of a pore mushroom. Microscopic spores fall from these pores and drift away in the wind.

Mushrooms produce enormous numbers of these microscopic spores which, in a way, are like seeds in that they may eventually produce other mushrooms. The common horse mushroom (*Agaricus arvensis*), for example, may produce 16 billion spores, while a large bracket fungus growing on the side of a tree may, in one summer, produce more than five trillion spores! These spores are carried away by winds but it is fortunate that very few ever germinate and grow into mushrooms. If they did, there would soon be no room for any other form of life on our planet!

The life history of a mushroom is quite interesting. When a spore germinates it produces a fine network of threads called *hyphae* (singular: *hypha*). These hyphae grow through the soil obtaining nourishment by absorbing food which is dissolved by enzymes they secrete. Eventually, this mass of threadlike hyphae may extend through a considerable area of soil. When conditions are right, all the food that has been stored in the underground

The undersurfaces of most mushrooms have radiating gills, between which the spores are produced. The colors of these spores are important in mushroom identification. They may be white, pink, brown, purple, or black.

If a mushroom cap is removed from the stem and carefully placed on a piece of paper, the spores falling on the paper will make a "spore pattern" like this. Be sure to cover the cap and the paper with an inverted jar or bowl to keep air currents from blowing the spores away as they fall from between the gills.

hyphae begins to flow toward one point where a typical mushroom is formed and pushes up through the soil. After shedding its spores it dies. Yet some fungi, such as the bracket fungi, often found growing on the sides of trees, do not die at once but may live for a long while.

Most large, fleshy fungi, such as mushrooms, are a favorite food of many animals. Tree squirrels devour them eagerly and insects of many kinds will eat nothing else. The larvae of fungus gnats (family Mycetophilidae) specialize in fungus food. While these insects merely feed upon fungi wherever they can find them, there are other insects that actually grow their own fungus as a source of food. One kind of insect with this habit are the ambrosia beetles (family Scolytidae) which excavate tunnels in living trees. There are several different kinds but each kind cultivates its own special fungus. When a female ambrosia beetle leaves the parent tree and tunnels into a new tree to establish a colony she takes a "start" of fungus or *ambrosia* with her. Within the tree she deposits the bit of fungus which thrives upon the damp, living wood. The female beetle then lays her eggs and she and her young feed upon the fungus garden. Trees in which the beetles have established their tunnels are often injured, both by the tunnels and by the fungus that stains the wood.

Even more interesting are the famous leaf-cutting ants (*Atta* ants) of tropical countries and southern United States that excavate large cavities in the ground and then make expeditions into the surrounding forest where they gather fragments of leaves. The leaf fragments are carried back into the nest and used as a compost upon which fungus is grown. It is an amazing sight to watch a foraging column of these leaf-cutting ants hurrying home, each with a section of leaf in its jaws. Since the leaves are carried over their heads these ants are also known as parasol ants. Within the underground nest cavity, which may be the size of a watermelon, the worker ants deposit their leaves upon

48

This picture of a cluster of Claudopus mushrooms shows the radiating gills on their undersides. This mushroom grows on logs and has a disagreeable odor. It produces pink spores.

This shelf fungus grew on a stump. It measured nearly three feet across.

Insects of several different kinds cultivate fungi for food. Shown here is a Trachymyrmex *ant working in its underground fungus garden. These little fungus growers are found in almost all parts of the United States.*

the mass of gray fungus. This is the fungus garden and here certain other ants, of smaller size, toil continuously, cutting the leaves up into tiny bits and placing them in the growing fungus to nourish it and keep it growing. Naturally, the larger ants that go out of the nest in search of leaves accidentally bring in "foreign" fungi and one of the duties of the smaller ants is to "weed out" these foreign fungi. Here in their cool, deep "mushroom" cellars the ants toil continuously in the darkness, tending their fungus garden. Here and there over its surface are produced tiny clumplike growths called *bromatia*. It is upon these that the ants feed; they do not eat the threadlike mycelia of the fungus. It is a strange fact that this ant fungus has been cultivated by the ants so long that it cannot grow by itself. If the ants desert a fungus garden, the fungus dies.

While the large *Atta* ants occur only in the warmer lands, you may be interested to know that there are small cousins of these ants that live as far north as New England. These are the *Trach-*

ymyrmex ants which gather small bits of plant material and use it as a compost for their small fungus gardens. These little ants are strange looking, being covered with minute warts or spines. Their underground cavities are about the size of an orange.

In Africa there are termites that also cultivate fungus. One kind is named *Macrotermes natalensis* and it chews up wood particles and uses them as a fungus compost. In the case of the termites, however, there is an interesting difference in habits. Fungus-raising ants of all castes feed upon the *bromatia* but, in the case of the termites, only the chosen few have this privilege, this choice food being reserved for the kings, queens and young termites.

It may seem strange that some insects have developed the habit of cultivating fungi and no other kind of plants. But it is perhaps understandable when one considers that fungi are small

This bracket fungus (Polyporus) grows on dead wood. The concentric bands are caused by successive periods of growth. Spores are produced in pores on the undersurfaces.

and easily grown in the dark tunnels where the insects live. There are few more remarkable things in nature.

It was previously mentioned that certain luminous molds sometimes grow in rotting wood, causing it to shine in the dark. There are actually more than fifty different kinds of luminous fungi in the world and many of these are mushrooms. One of the largest mushrooms with this characteristic is the jack-o'-lantern mushroom, known to botanists as *Clitocybe illudens*. It often reaches a diameter of five inches and grows in clumps on stumps or logs. It is poisonous to humans, containing poisonous *muscarin*, the same substance found in the deadly *Amanita* mushrooms. In the darkness, it glows with an orange-colored light. Other luminous mushrooms occur in Europe, and in Japan there is a large kind called the "moonlight mushroom" that grows on the trunks of dead beech trees. The light given off by various luminous fungi is of different colors; it may be orange, yellow, blue, or greenish. On the island of Yap, in the Pacific

These tiny Marasmius *mushrooms grew on a dead twig in the Great Smoky Mountains. They are also found on dead leaves, logs, and on the ground.*

This golden Cantharellus *mushroom grows in deep forests. Another golden mushroom, the jack-o'-lantern* (Clitocybe illudens), *shines in the dark and is poisonous.*

Ocean, there occurs a kind of brightly luminous fungus that is often used as hair ornaments by the women during moonlight dances.

Now and then, large circular rings of mushrooms appear overnight on lawns and often cause considerable comment and wonder. In former years, people, knowing little about the natural growth processes of fungi, often attached supernatural interpretations to these so-called "fairy rings." It was believed that the mushrooms grew where fairies had danced in the moonlight. This is such a charming fantasy that it is rather sad to discredit it.

The fairy-ring mushroom, scientifically known as *Marasmius oreades,* occurs in many parts of the world, including Europe, Asia and Africa, as well as here in our own country. As in all mushrooms, the above-ground mushroom is merely the fruiting or spore-producing stage of the fungus plant. Mushrooms, as we have seen, live upon dead organic matter and do not possess green chlorophyll for manufacture of their own foods as do most other plants. People have always seemed to realize vaguely that

53

there was something unusual about mushrooms, which accounts for the many superstitions and erroneous beliefs that have grown up concerning them.

A fairy ring begins as a small ring produced when the spores from one individual mushroom fall to the ground, germinate, and begin the production of the typical, underground *mycelium* or threadlike growth. When spores fall from the mushrooms, making up this first, small circle, a somewhat larger circle of mycelia is produced which eventually gives rise to another, still larger, ring of mushrooms. Thus, year by year the circle becomes larger and larger until it may be fifty or more feet in diameter. The growth pattern of these fungi has been compared to the expanding ripples made on water when a stone is tossed into a pond. Large rings are the result of many successive generations of mushrooms in which each generation extended the circle outward a little farther. In one case it was estimated that 600 years had been required to create a large fairy ring. These strange fungus rings appear so suddenly and often in such perfect form that it is difficult to believe that some outside agency is not responsible. Sometimes the circles are incomplete; in fact, mere portions of circles are more common than complete rings. The species mentioned above is the most common one that grows in the form of fairy rings but there are other kinds with similar habits of growth. The true fairy-ring mushroom is edible but some of the others that grow in rings are poisonous.

Another common type of "mushroom" are the puffball fungi (*Calvatia*) often found growing in meadows and other places. Like ordinary mushrooms, they push up out of the ground and many often reach enormous size. One specimen was once seen that measured more than five feet in circumference. This is unusual, of course, since most of them are only a few inches in diameter. When freshly emerged from the soil their interiors are white but they gradually turn brown and become filled with spores. It is estimated that a large puffball may produce nearly ten trillion

Fairy-ring mushrooms often grow in ringlike groups on lawns. Year by year these fairy rings become larger and larger.

spores. In this stage they are not edible. As the puffball matures, one or more openings appear in its walls through which the spores escape and blow away. Usually, the opening is at the top and if the puffball is squeezed, a cloud of brown spores is forced out.

One often finds, in more or less sandy situations, strange star-shaped objects that are obviously some type of plant growth. Actually, these are a type of fungus closely related to the puff-ball mushroom, though they do not grow to the enormous size of the large puffballs. A species often seen is *Geaster hydrometricus.* The name *Geaster* comes, appropriately, from two Greek words, *geo* and *aster*, meaning "earth star." Altogether there are about twenty different species or kinds.

When earth-stars first appear above the ground they look like small puffballs about an inch in diameter. As they mature, how-ever, their outside layer splits into a number of segments, begin-

55

When mature, puffballs release their spores through open-
ings in their tops. If one is squeezed, a cloud of brown
spores is ejected. Normally, these spores are carried away
by winds to new locations where they germinate, producing
new puffballs.

ning at the top. These segments then peel downward like the skin of an orange, exposing the spherical inner wall. This is gray or brown and a small, irregular opening then appears at the top, out of which are ejected enormous numbers of brown, microscopic spores which drift away in the air. Some of these spores may give rise to other earth-stars. The thing that is especially interesting about these unusual fungi, however, is the fact that the outer skin sections which peel downward away from the sphere are highly sensitive to moisture. In dry weather they remain curled up around the spherical spore case but, if a rain comes, they uncurl and expand to such an extent that the entire structure is lifted off the ground and rests upon the tips of the sections like spiders. In this open position the fungus resembles a many-pointed star.

If one of these earth-stars is carried indoors and allowed to dry completely, its segments will slowly curl up around the spore sac, but if it is placed in a shallow saucer of water the

Earth-stars are a type of puffball in which the outer
wall peels downward in sections, exposing the spore
sac. Clouds of brown spores escape through the small
opening in the center.

Here you see how an earth-star is lifted off of damp ground by its spidery
"legs." When the specimen at the left was placed on damp sand the skin
segments bent downward, lifting it up. The specimen at the right, on dry
sand, still has its skin segments curled up around it.

hygroscopic or water-absorbing nature of the sections will cause them to rapidly absorb water and bend outward and downward. If it is again dried, its sections will curl up around the spore sac and the process may be repeated as often as it is dried and moistened. Due to the fact that this fungus is so sensitive to changes in humidity it was once called the "poor man's weather glass." This characteristic also gave it the specific name, *hydro-metricus*, which means "water measurer."

We might speculate as to the reasons behind the unique behavior of these fungi. While maturing, earth-stars remain partly buried in the soil but, when mature, the sections peel downward, lifting them above the level of the surrounding earth, where they will remain dry and where winds can pick up and carry away their spores.

Many people have heard of truffles without knowing that they are a type of mushroom that grows entirely underground. They are common in European countries and have been considered delicacies since early Greek and Roman days. The chief diffi-culty, as you might guess, is the finding of these fungi since they

Puffballs are quite common everywhere. This kind (Calbovista subsculpta) is found in the western mountains. Some puffballs reach large size. They are all edible when first appearing above the ground.

Bird's-nest fungi are fairly common on rotten wood or decaying leaves. They are among the most unusual of all small fungi. The spores are contained in the "eggs" which are splashed out of the "nests" during rains. At first the "nests" are covered by a thin membrane, but this disappears, revealing the "eggs." There are several different kinds of bird's-nest fungi. This one is Cyathus striatus. *(See next photograph)*

grow underground. Long ago this problem was solved by training dogs or pigs to locate them by scent. Such animals are called "truffle hounds."

Last but not least in interest are the peculiar little bird's-nest fungi sometimes found growing on decayed wood or, even, on the ground. These little fungi belong to family Nidulariaceae. They cannot be mistaken for any other fungus since, as their name indicates, they resemble rows or clusters of tiny, cuplike birds' nests complete with eggs. These "eggs" contain the fungus spores. What is of special interest, however, is the manner by which the fungus scatters its spores. The cups are very symmetrically formed, a fact that makes one wonder if this serves

An adhesive thread from each "egg" of a bird's-nest fungus enables it to attach itself to a grass blade or a twig from which it hangs suspended. If this is eaten by an animal, the spores are released and, later, germinate on the ground or on rotten wood.

some purpose. For a long while botanists were mystified, but the function of the cups or "nests" is now known. These cups are so designed that when drops of rain fall into them the spore-filled "eggs," or *periodioles,* are splashed out and sail through the air, sometimes as far as seven feet away! Attached to each "egg" is a sticky thread or cord. If the "egg," sailing through the air, strikes a leaf or a plant stem it attaches itself to it by the sticky thread and hangs suspended in the air. Now if a cow, deer, or other leaf-eating animal should eat the leaf, the attached *periodiole,* or "egg," is swallowed along with it. The fungus spores contained in the "egg" are not destroyed by the animal's digestive system and so the spores, now liberated from their case, pass out of the animal and germinate. This is an effective method of obtaining a free ride to a new location since the animal may, in the meantime, have traveled a considerable distance.

Some of the most interesting and unusual kinds of fungi can be found on fallen logs and trees, especially after periods of wet weather. Many of these rotten-wood fungi are very colorful.

CHAPTER 4

Slime-molds: Plants or Animals?

*M*ost of us think that we can tell a plant from an animal, and usually we can. Certainly, we can tell that a rabbit is an animal and that a cabbage is a plant. But if we could go back far enough in time we would come to the place where the ways divided, where the plants followed one fork in the road while the animals took the other. In the dim beginning there were simple forms of life, but they were probably neither plant nor animal. Even today, there is no sharp line of distinction between some simple forms of plant and animal life, and botanists and zoologists do not always agree as to which is a plant and which is an animal. The strange slime-molds are a good example.

The slime-molds are a form of life that lies in the twilight zone between the plant and animal kingdoms. While they are now usually classified as plants, there was a time not too long ago when they were claimed by the zoologists. Proof of this is in their former name, *Mycetozoa,* which means "fungus animal." Even though they are now usually called *Myxomycetes* or "slime fungi," the older name is still used by some biologists, so the matter is seemingly still unsettled.

If you turn over decaying logs, especially after a spell of wet weather, you are apt to see masses of slimy material several inches across on or in the wood. These are slime-molds and they may be red, brown, yellow, or white, depending upon the kind.

61

If you are lucky, and examine one of these slime-molds carefully, you may notice that it is not a uniform mass of slime but that there are strands or "veins" running through it. You will also notice that there is a "leading edge" as it spreads out over the wood. Now, if you will stick a pin in the wood at the front edge of the slime-mold and then look at it again an hour or so later, you will find it has crept over the surface beyond the pin. This is a characteristic of slime-molds; they "flow" or creep slowly along like giant amoebae. This is their method of feeding. As they move along they surround and absorb food particles. It is this method of creeping along as they feed that, more than anything else, has led some biologists to classify them as animals.

While we usually think of plants as being made up of individual cells, slime-molds have no cell walls; they are simply masses of living protoplasm. These strange "creatures" feed upon bacteria, yeasts, fungus spores and bits of dead leaves. Their method of feeding has been compared, by Dr. John Tyler Bonner of Princeton University, to a flock of sheep. A slime-mold, when "grazing," spreads out over the wood, its protoplasm streaming along in "veins." When the food has all been consumed, the slimy masses of protoplasm flow back together again. Not only do slime-molds move along but there is a rhythmic flow of protoplasm within the creeping slime-mold. It tends to flow in one direction for awhile, then flows backward for a minute or so. But, since it flows longer in the forward direction, the mold slowly moves along over the surface of the rotten wood.

One question that has always puzzled biologists is how this uniform mass of living protoplasm coordinates or governs its actions. How does one part "know" what the other part is doing? When one portion of a slime-mold begins flowing in a certain direction, how do all portions of it get the message? The answers to these interesting questions are, at present, rather hazy, but apparently slime-molds secrete chemical substances that regulate or control their activities just as the growth activities of

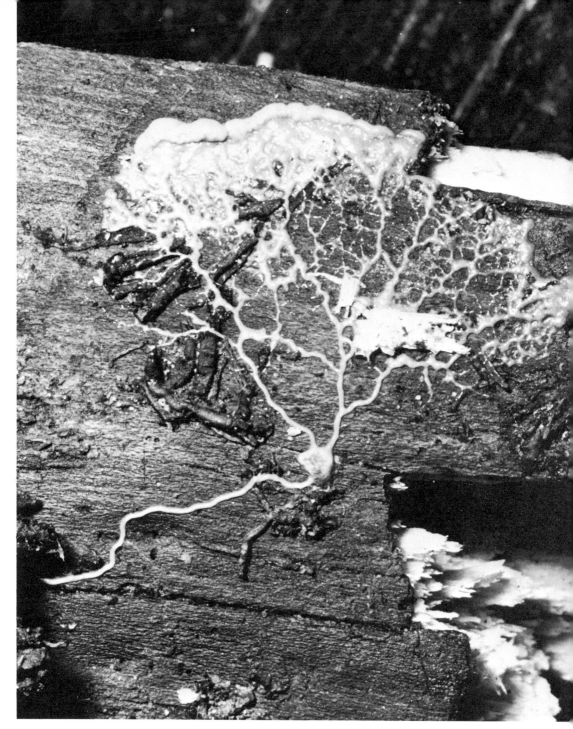

This is the creeping or "animal" stage of a slime-mold. The forward edge is toward the top. The mass of protoplasm or living slime flows along over rotten wood, feeding as it goes.

Sporangia of Stemonitis *are nearly an inch tall. This slime-mold is common on rotting wood.*

higher plants are controlled by chemical regulators called *auxins*.

A slime-mold creeps over damp wood for a time but when conditions are right it rather suddenly begins transforming itself into another stage. If you wish to observe this interesting transformation you can do so by placing the piece of rotting wood containing a slime-mold in a large jar where it will stay damp. (The transformation may be speeded up if it is allowed to dry out some.) The first indication that the slime-mold is about to change into the "plant" stage is the appearance of small clumps on its surface. Slowly these become higher and higher and at last they change into dark-colored spore-bearing structures called *sporangia*. The change takes several hours. These sporangia are of many rather amazing forms and they vary according to the kind of slime-mold, of which there are about 400 different kinds. If you will use a hand lens to examine dead leaves, dead twigs, rotten logs or pieces of damp wood you will probably find some clusters of these sporangia. Since they are very small you will have to look carefully.

Even though these sporangia are very tiny — few are taller than one-eighth inch — they have interesting forms. Some look like tiny bird cages complete with stands, others are in the form of feather-like plumes, while still others look like cones filled with red cotton candy. These sporangia are filled with microscopic spores which, when dry, are carried away by breezes. If these spores alight on decaying wood and, if conditions of moisture and temperature are favorable, they germinate, each one forming a cell having one or two whiplike projections or *flagella*. These cells swim about in water or moisture for awhile by means of their flagella. Eventually they lose these swimming organs and begin creeping about like the single-celled animals known as amoebae. In time these grow into typical slime-molds. Con-

Physarum sporangia are often found on logs. They are about a quarter inch tall and gray in color. The heads contain many microscopic spores.

These Arcyria *sporangia are very attractive. They look like red masses of cotton candy in cones.*

Here is a stalked slime-mold sporangia of Dictydium. *It resembles a tiny bird cage complete with stand. Within is the ball of spores. When breezes tumble this spore ball about in the case, the spores are sifted out and blow away. Natural size: one-eighth inch tall.*

ditions favorable to the growth of slime-molds include abundant moisture, warmth and dim light. Slime-mold spores may remain alive and capable of germination for more than fifty years.

While the sporangia stages of slime-molds are very small, they are usually more easily found than the creeping stages since the latter are usually located deep inside logs. However, if logs are rolled over they may often be found on the damp undersides.

Most slime-molds are of no economic importance to us; they are of interest chiefly because of their peculiar forms and life histories. There are, however, a few kinds that attack plants. One of these, *Plasmodiophora brassicae*, attacks the roots of cabbage, causing a disease known as cabbage club-root.

Slime-molds in their sporangia stages make unusually interesting subjects for natural history collections. While perhaps not as spectacular as butterfly collections, they are indeed different. Pieces of rotten wood with attached clumps of sporangia may be glued to the bottoms of pill boxes and the names and other data recorded on the lids. A small hand lens of about 10-power is needed for their study. Such collections will last almost indefinitely.

These are crustose lichens that grow closely attached to rocks and the bark of trees. They often look like smears of paint.

CHAPTER 5

What Lichens Are Like

$\mathcal{T}$here are many strange plants in the world and some of their habits seem to have come directly out of science fiction. But of all the world's plants the lichens are probably the most unusual. They are small plants of little economic importance and do not appear, at first glance, to be very interesting. Everyone has seen lichens; some kinds form crustlike or mosslike growths over rocks and trees, while others grow on the ground. However, it is not the appearance of lichens that makes them unique among plants; it is their manner of growth. A lichen is not just a plant; it is two plants living together in a sort of mutual benefit society. How it all started botanists do not know; neither do they know quite how to go about naming them. The word "lichen" is of Greek origin, meaning "leprous," in reference to the fact that these plants form scurfy growths on tree bark. While the word was first applied to liverworts, the Greek medical writer, Dioscorides, about 2,000 years ago, recommended lichens for leprosy and the name came to belong to the plants we know as lichens.

A lichen consists of a fungus and an alga united into a single structure having all the characteristics of one plant. It begins life, grows and reproduces itself as if it were a single plant. Each of the plants making up this partnership is a simple and different form of plant life. One is a fungus and the other is an alga.

To plant taxonomists — botanists who classify plants — lichens are a problem. Botanists have tidy habits and like to classify all plants in precise detail, giving each one a special, scientific name. It is by these scientific names that plants are known to botanists in all parts of the world. In the case of lichens, there was no problem until 1867 when a Swiss botanist named Simon Schwendener decided that lichens were not one plant but two plants closely associated together. This made things complicated since the question at once arose as to whether or not each plant should have a separate name. Some botanists maintained, and still do, that the fungus should be given one name and the alga another name. It has been proposed that the fungus be designated by adding *myces* (the Greek word for fungus) to the present name of the lichen. Thus, the fungus in the common lichen, *Parmelia*, often found growing on trees, would become *Parmeliomyces*.

As far as the green algae partners of the lichen fungi are concerned, the matter is less complicated since they already have scientific names. These algae can, and do, live separately and so have been classified separately. The fungi, on the other hand, are dependent upon the algae and cannot live without them and are never found growing in nature without their algae partners. Thus, it is possible that at some time in the future when the relationships between lichen fungi and their algae are better understood, botanists may revise their method of naming them. But, for the present, we must follow the usual method of giving each lichen one name as though each kind was one plant and not made up of two. Each kind or species of lichen is made up of the same alga and the same fungus, and its form and coloration is just as uniform as in any other plant.

Just how or when this strange partnership began, botanists do not know. From a geological standpoint, it is usually believed that lichens are rather recent. Their fossils have been found in amber and in peat beds that are only a few million years old. Both the fungi and the algae originally lived separately upon tree bark or rocks but, in time, some fungi "discovered" that they

Lichens spread their creeping growths over boulders and cliffs, slowly etching away the stone and creating soil where other plants can grow.

could get along better if they surrounded a few of the green algal cells and absorbed some of their food. Thus, these fungi actually became parasitic upon the algae. As time slowly passed, there developed between the two kinds of plants a certain degree of mutual benefit.

In nature, there are many other instances where two plants (or two animals, or a plant and an animal) cooperate for their mutual benefit. This is called a *symbiosis*, from the Greek, meaning "living together." In the case of a lichen, the fungus obtains food and moisture from the alga, while the alga is protected by the fungus covering and is furnished with minerals that the fungus obtains from the bark or stone upon which it grows.

If one carefully dissects a lichen under a microscope, both the colorless fungus strands and the green, spherical algal cells can be seen very easily. The outside surfaces of the lichen are com-

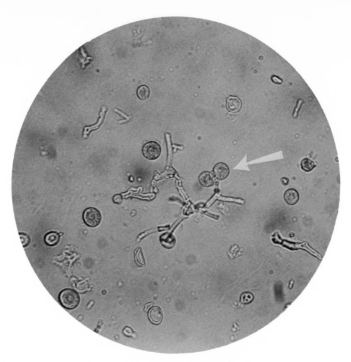

If a lichen is broken into fragments and examined under a microscope, its inner structure can be seen. The transparent strands are fungus mycelia, while the algal cells (arrow) are seen as spheres. Note how the mycelia are attached to the algal cells from which they obtain their nourishment.

posed of fungus tissue within which the algal cells are well protected. When the lichen is dry it appears to be brown or some other dull color; this is because the green algal cells are hidden within the fungus tissue. It is during periods of wet or rainy weather that lichens take on their most colorful hues. Then the fungus absorbs moisture and becomes transparent, allowing the colorful alga to show through it. While lichen algae require moist conditions they are not types that actually live in water. Without the fungus they are able to thrive alone on damp soil, tree bark or rocks, especially if there are periods of rain or if the air is humid. These algae belong to two groups, the blue-green algae *(Cyanophyta)* and the common green algae *(Chlorophyta).* While many lichens grow most luxuriantly in damp situations, there are other kinds, as we shall see, that grow on desert rocks or in cold, Arctic climates. Of all the world's plant life, the lichens are the most widely distributed, often being found in places where no other plants are able to survive.

We now turn our attention to another interesting problem involving these unusual little members of the plant kingdom. Since lichens are composed of two plants, how do they reproduce themselves? Actually, lichens reproduce themselves in several ways. First, let us consider their reproduction by sexual means. Most of the fungi associated with algae in lichens are sac or cup fungi (*Ascomycetes*) which produce microscopic sacs, each of which usually contains eight spores produced by union of sex cells arising from nearby branches of the fungus strands. These spore sacs are usually located in shallow, cup-shaped fruiting bodies on the lichen. When mature, these spores are discharged during periods of wet weather. During such wet conditions the fungal cells become filled with water and considerable internal pressure develops. This causes the spores to be discharged into the air.

The fungus in the lichen reproduces by means of microscopic spores. Shown here are such spores greatly magnified.

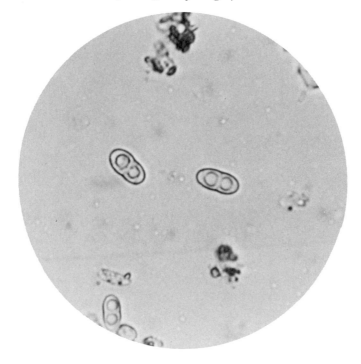

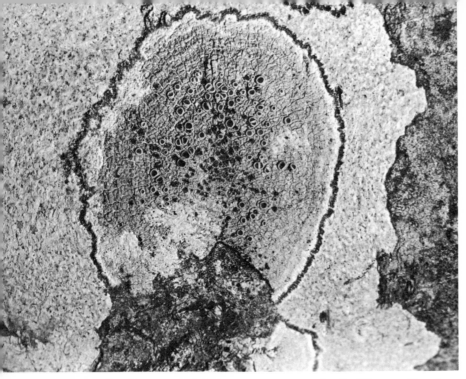

This Lecanora *lichen grows on tree bark. The small, white-rimmed discs are spore-producing cups.*

If these fungus spores alight upon a favorable site they germinate like tiny seeds, producing a typical network of fungus threads or *mycelia*. During this stage of its life the fungus absorbs its nourishment and water from the surface upon which it grows. It grows alone and has no green algal cells to manufacture food for it. In time, however, the fungus strands are apt to come in contact with its own particular kind of green algal cells which are usually found growing in similar situations. When this occurs, the fungus strands surround the algal cells and form little attachments to them. From this point on the fungus grows faster and changes its way of life, becoming dependent upon the alga for its food supply. Slowly, it begins growing into the typical lichen form. Thus, we see that the lichen starts out in life on its own but later "captures" some algal cells and "enslaves" them. Perhaps here we have a clue to the origin of lichens; perhaps this is the way the cooperative habit originated in the first place.

The above is the sexual reproductive method of lichens, but

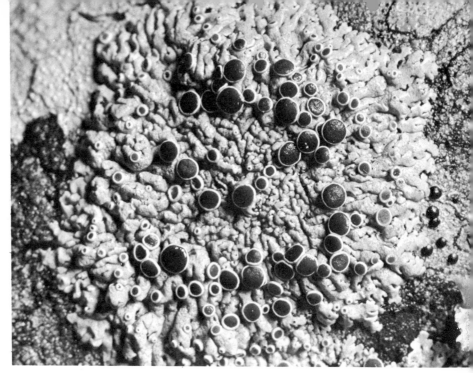

The star Physia *lichen spreads its growth on tree trunks. Its spores are also produced in discs or cups.*

there are other, more common, methods. Upon the surface of the lichen are produced tiny clumps of fungus containing a few algal cells. These clumps are called *soredia* and they break loose and are blown away by winds or are carried by rains to other locations where they settle down and grow into typical lichens. Still another reproductive method is by fragmentation. Dry lichens are very brittle during dry weather and small pieces of them are apt to break off and blow away. If such fragments lodge on moist surfaces they attach themselves and grow.

While lichen fungi and algae normally live together as units, each one can be grown separately in the laboratory upon suitable nutrient media in much the same way as bacteria are grown. It is not surprising that the algae can be artificially cultivated because they often live independently anyway, but it is very interesting that lichen fungi can be grown without their cooperative algae. When these fungi are grown alone on culture media they develop into small patches of tangled fungus threads but never develop into the usual lichen form; neither do they produce spores. Evidently the alga partner is necessary for normal development.

Before leaving the subject of the alga-fungus partnerships of lichens we might mention that there are a few lichens that apparently are not satisfied with just one kind of alga but have "adopted" yet a second kind. This second "guest" alga is always of the blue-green family and, since some of these algae have the ability to "fix" or absorb nitrogen from the air, it is possible that is the reason the lichens have adopted them. The blue-green algae supply them with nitrogen which is so important to the growth of all plants.

Lichenologists — botanists who specialize in lichens — have made many observations and studies of the relationships between lichens and the places in which they live. Biologists like to have special names for everything, so the study of plants and animals in relation to their environments, or places they live, is called *ecology*. Lichen ecology is very precise; they will not flourish under some conditions such as those that prevail in or near large cities where smog and other toxic materials are present in the air. As a result, many kinds of lichens have disappeared from such areas. This has been especially true of the British Isles and in highly industrialized areas of Europe. It is indeed strange that these small plants, which can survive Arctic and Antarctic cold as well as the heat of the world's great deserts, should be unable to cope with comparatively minute amounts of poisonous materials in the air.

Until the coming of man the lichens were able to survive almost any condition that Nature could devise. Probably, of all plant life, the lichens can stand the greatest extremes of both temperature and humidity. In one experiment, dry lichens were exposed to a temperature of 434°F. This, you will recall, is more than twice that of boiling water. The lichens were exposed to this heat for seven hours, at the end of which time they began

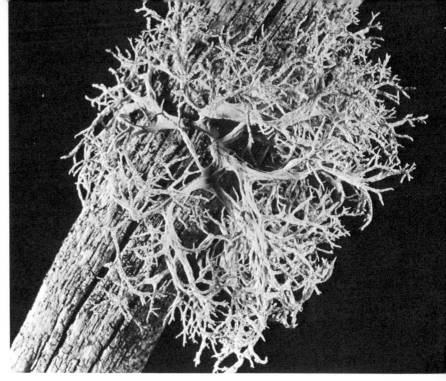

This is the golden lichen of western mountains. It grows on dead pine limbs at high altitudes and is a beautiful shade of bright gold.

growing again! On the other hand, dry lichens can also survive exposure to extreme cold, a characteristic that enables them to live in polar regions. While they can survive such severe conditions when their moisture content is very low, it is probable that they would be killed if they were to be exposed to either high or low temperatures while their cells were filled with water.

Probably the one thing that has enabled lichens to survive in the world is their ability to grow when conditions are favorable and to become dormant when conditions become unfavorable. If you observe these plants in the heat of late summer when no rain has fallen for several weeks you will notice that they are dry and brittle and that their colors are dull. On the other hand, when periods of wet weather occur the lichens take on new life and literally glow with vivid coloration. This is because of the moisture they rapidly absorb. It has been found that the water content of lichens varies from as low as only 2 per cent to as high as 300 per cent of their own weight. Not only do they absorb water from falling rain but they can also absorb it from the atmosphere.

Plants, such as lichens, that survive under adverse conditions usually grow very slowly. The growth of many lichens is so slow that increase in size from year to year is hardly noticeable and some of them require eight or ten years to produce fruiting cups. Since lichens grow when conditions are favorable and become dormant during adverse periods, they live for a long while. It is possible that some kinds may continue growth for thousands of years on rocks in Arctic regions where they are undisturbed.

We have already seen that the alga in the alga-fungus partnership of a lichen furnishes manufactured foods, but just what does the fungus contribute? This fungus absorbs and holds moisture in large quantities but the alga could do this alone, though perhaps not as efficiently. As lichens grow, the fungus produces minute *hyphae* or rootlike growths that anchor it to the surface

This bright golden Rhizocarpon *lichen grew on a boulder beneath the towering Teton Mountains of Wyoming. It was an inch in diameter.*

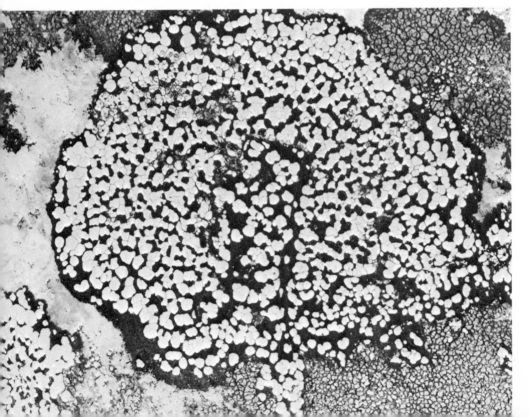

This greenish-yellow old-man's-beard lichen (Usnea) is an example of a fruticose lichen. It hangs from tree limbs like Spanish moss which, incidentally, is neither a moss nor a lichen. Actually, Spanish moss is an air-plant closely related to pineapple.

upon which it grows. Biologists are not in agreement as to whether these "roots" are important in absorbing minerals. In some kinds, such as old-man's-beard lichen, which grows on tree limbs, there is very little attachment, so very little food is obtained directly from the bark. While tree-living lichens are not parasites like mistletoes and do not injure trees, they evidently do obtain something from the bark. Those that creep over rocks definitely obtain minerals from them. Lichens do not usually flourish on dead trees and they do not grow upon some kinds of living trees. Apparently the bark of some trees contain substances that make lichen growth impossible. This is obvious if one walks through a mixed forest growth. Some trees are covered with lichens while others are bare. Beech trees, for example, do not harbor many lichens since they shed their outer bark layers quite rapidly and there is simply not time enough for slow-growing lichens to develop. The same is true of white oak.

Lichens growing upon rocks and cliffs produce acids which slowly etch away the surfaces and speed up weathering processes. Other kinds secrete gelatin-like substances that dry upon hard surfaces and cause them to crack off in flakes. Old church windows are often etched and pitted in this way by lichen growth. During growth, lichens excrete or give off carbon dioxide and this, too, etches away stone. As a result, lichens are important in the conversion of bare rocks to soil and have, without doubt, had a great deal to do with preparing places where other plants can later grow. As rock particles are loosened and fall away, they collect in crevices and depressions where mosses and ferns begin growth. The roots of these small plants, in turn, crack off more rock particles and collect more soil and rock debris. In time, larger pockets are formed where the seeds of flowering plants, such as violets, can sprout and grow. Thus, step by step, the way is paved for more and larger plants in the chain of life. In a way, lichens are pioneer plants that often prepare the way for other kinds of plant life. This, we might consider, is the role of many kinds of lichens in Nature's scheme of plant growth.

Lichenology, the study of lichens, is a difficult science and there are only a few people in the world who are authorities on their identification. This is probably the reason why these interesting little plants have received so little attention in popular books on natural history. Another thing that complicates matters is the fact that only a few of them have common names. The precise identification of most lichens requires a study of their structural details under a microscope at high magnification. This

The first forms of plant life to grow on cooled lava that once flowed from volcanoes are lichens. The Craters of the Moon area of Idaho is a vast expanse formed by volcanic lava. The black surface is now covered by creeping lichens and some mosses. A few scattered shrubs and flowering plants also eke out existences on the rocky landscape.

is a thing that few amateurs are either willing or equipped to do. What the beginner needs is close-up pictures, and few publications on lichens have many. The most extensive publication on American lichens is *The Lichen Flora of the United States* by Bruce Fink, but while there are more than 400 pages, there are only a few pictures. Yet there are about 15,000 different kinds of lichens in the world.

As a result, we do the best we can with pictures of common kinds and have to be satisfied, in many cases, with their technical names. Fortunately, these names are not difficult and often have pleasing sounds, such as *Cladonia, Bacidia, Lecidea, Sticta, Ramalina,* and *Cetraria*. In this age of science we should become accustomed to using such technical names.

In general, lichens fall into three groups, depending upon their manners of growth. These are as follows:

Crustose lichens

These grow in the form of hard crusts on rocks and the bark of trees. They grow so tightly against the surface that they cannot be pulled off and some of them look like smears of gray or greenish paint.

Foliose lichens

These are leaflike in form and grow on trees or rocks. Often their edges are crinkled and raised above the surface. Rock tripe lichen, for example, is a dark green kind having its edges curled up so as to expose their black undersurfaces. Sometimes the upper surfaces of these lichens are covered with cuplike, spore-bearing structures. *Parmelia* is another common example.

Fruticose lichens

This type is easily identified. They grow erect from the ground or hang from tree limbs. Usually they are branching. Good examples are reindeer moss which grows on the ground, and old-man's-beard which hangs from trees. They are best described as being "shrubby."

The colors of lichens are usually of but little aid in identification even though some are quite pretty. Some are golden while others are green or blue-green. One of our most attractive common lichens is the ground-living kind often known as "British soldiers" because of the scarlet tips or "heads" of its stalks. It is a *Cladonia* closely related to reindeer moss.

Lichens are very easy to collect and study. Almost any large forest tree is host to many kinds. If you can locate a recently fallen tree you are in luck, since the upper branches are often clothed with many kinds. Bits of bark to which the lichens are attached can be chopped out and kept as dried specimens for many years. Collections can be stored in trays or boxes.

This Ramalina *lichen is an example of a* fruticose *lichen. These lichens grow loosely attached to tree limbs, as does this one, or erect from the ground.*

This dog-lichen is a good example of a foliose lichen. Such lichens are of leaflike form and grow on trees and rocks.

On high mountain peaks of the West, where almost Arctic conditions prevail, lichens are found growing on stone. No other plants can survive the cold. Shown here is a high peak of the Teton Mountains of Wyoming where snows never melt completely, but where lichens grow abundantly.

CHAPTER 6

Lichens, the Pioneers

$\mathcal{T}$he late Vilhjalmur Stefansson, the noted Arctic explorer, often spoke of the Arctic region as a friendly place where many plants and animals, as well as men, find suitable habitats. To be sure, it is a land of ice and cold and of long, polar nights, yet, during its brief summers, more than a hundred different kinds of plants come into flower, produce seeds and die. Considering the severe climate, this is very remarkable and demonstrates the fact that some plants can live and grow where least expected. Of all the plants that grow in the regions beyond the Arctic and Antarctic Circles, however, the lichens and a few other simple plants, such as mosses and liverworts, seem best adapted.

The Arctic region is much richer in fauna and flora than the Antarctic, largely because all of the great land masses of the Northern Hemisphere extend northward above the Arctic Circle. In the Southern Hemisphere, by contrast, there are vast stretches of cold, empty ocean between the nearest continents and the frozen land of Antarctica. Neither of the great southern continents—Africa and South America—reaches even close to the Antarctic Circle. As contrasted to the relatively abundant plant life of the Arctic, there are only three flowering plants native to the Antarctic. These are a small pink named *Colobanthus crassifolius* and two grasses, *Deschampsia parvula* and *D. elegantula*. In all the vast, dreary stretches of the Antarctic continent

85

there are no other flowering plants and these grow in only a few sheltered places, all of which are on the northern tip of the Antarctic Peninsula where it extends north of the Antarctic Circle. Thus, there are actually no flowers at all in Antarctica proper. Whereas small, shrubby trees, such as willows, grow on the tundra beyond the Arctic Circle, the nearest trees to Antarctica are those found on barren Tierra del Fuego, 700 miles to the north on the southernmost tip of South America.

Antarctica is a vast continent; it contains 5.5 million square miles of land, almost all of which is covered by glacial ice and hard-packed snow. The South Pole, itself, is covered by a layer of ice two miles in depth! Only about 3,000 square miles of Antarctica are ever exposed, even during the short, polar summers. It is almost completely cut off from the rest of the world. Surrounding its shores are masses of pack ice; beyond this stretches the cold expanse of empty ocean that no land animal could cross. As a result, there are no warm-blooded land animals at all in Antarctica. You will at once think of penguins, sea birds and seals, but these are sea animals, not land animals. By contrast, the Arctic has many land animals, including polar bears, wolves, foxes, rabbits, caribou and mouselike lemmings.

On the vast continent of Antarctica, which is larger than the United States in size, there are only a few native land animals of any kind, all of which are very tiny. The largest of these is a small, wingless gnat (*Belgica antarctica*) whose larvae breed in brackish pools near the coast. This same gnat is also found on Tierra del Fuego. How it got to Antarctica is unknown. The most numerous land creatures are springtail insects (*Collembola*) and some mites. The mites are pink in color and only one-hundredth of an inch long. These small creatures have been found at 6,000-foot elevations on mountains and at lower elevations only 309 miles from the South Pole where temperatures often plunge to 85°F. below zero. Here, upon exposed rocks, these tiny creatures live among mosses and lichens. Dr. Paul

Lichens cover these rocks on barren Anvers Island in Antarctica. In this bleak region few plants grow, most of which are mosses, lichens, and algae.

Siple, the noted Antarctic explorer, found lichens within 237 miles of the Pole. These plants are able to live and grow even though they are covered with ice and snow for ten months out of the year.

Just how these small plants and animals exist there is a mystery. Even at the height of Antarctic summers, temperatures are never warm. Evidently the sun heats the rocks sufficiently for a thin layer of warm air to form over them. Within this shallow zone of warmth the mosses and lichens are able to grow, but their growth is very slow, only a little each year. The air is very dry and both lichens and mosses can withstand very cold temperatures under such conditions. Thus, only a short distance from the Pole, live insects, mites and plants in what is probably the world's most inhospitable region. The growth of lichens also extends down below the ice where they apparently obtain enough sunlight through the glasslike ice to keep them alive.

There are many fresh-water ponds in Antarctica, which result from the melting of snow and glacial ice, but these ponds contain no snails, insects or fish. The highest form of animal life in these waters are small fairy shrimp (*Branchinecta granulosa*). The only other creatures in Antarctic ponds are minute rotifers and tardigrades which are similar to those found in any pond in our own country.

While lichens, which are composite plants made up of an alga and a fungus, seem able to live in Antarctica, there are very few free-living fungi. This is as one would suspect in such a climate. On the other hand, there are many kinds of algae and these grow upon the open ground as well as upon the snow at times. Blue-green algae in tremendous numbers often cover the face of Wilson Piedmont Glacier in Victoria Land which lies well within the Antarctic zone. All of the kinds of algae that grow in this area are apparently the same kinds found in warmer climates far to the north. Under certain conditions, during Antarctic summer, the snow becomes covered with algae of rosy colors. At times, many acres of snow take on a reddish hue from the presence of these minute plants.

Of all plant life in Antarctica, however, the lichens are by far the most abundant in both kinds and numbers. There are about 400 kinds, which is most remarkable when one considers the climate and the distance of the polar continent from other regions. Some Antarctic lichens are believed to be at least a thousand years old. The presence of this abundant lichen flora brings up an interesting question. How did they get there in the first place? So far, botanists do not know. They do know that, many millions of years ago, the climate of the Antarctic continent was more or less tropical. Fossilized remains of many trees have been discovered there. The first of these fossil trees to be found was that of a pine on Seymour Island, near the tip of Palmer Peninsula in the summer of 1892-93. Later, Sir Ernest Shackleton and his exploring party found another pine log and

In spite of the cold and the long Antarctic winters, lichens grow abundantly on the rocks on Anvers Island. Here Dr. I. Mackenzie Lamb of Harvard University, well-known authority on lichens, studies foliose or "leafy" lichens (rock tripe) on a rocky hillside. Antarctic mosses are seen in the background.

coal deposits near Beardmore Glacier which faces the Ross Ice Shelf and which is not too far from the South Pole. Fossilized leaves and twigs have been found, and petrified logs of ancient trees up to 18 inches in diameter were found at Mount Weaver

These lichens (Cladonia deformis) *were photographed at the edge of the snow at an elevation of nearly 9,000 feet in the Rocky Mountains.*

which protrudes up through the ice only a short distance from the Pole. From the presence of these and other fossils we now know that this frozen land was once warm and that it had deep forests where many kinds of plant life flourished. Probably it was once a pleasant land where one could have strolled through groves of palms and ancient ferns. Perhaps there were even dinosaurs in these forests that covered Antarctica 165 million years ago. What amazing changes have occurred!

It is possible that the lichens that now grow in this icy land are survivors from the ancient days when the land was warmer. Perhaps, as the climate became colder and colder, they, of all the luxuriant plant life that lived there, were able to adapt themselves and survive. On the other hand, it is possible that the spores of lichen fungi have been carried there by winds from warmer lands. Alighting and germinating near green alga cells, they may have re-established the partnership and developed into lichens. Certainly, it is true that many of the Antarctic lichens are the same kinds found elsewhere.

We have now seen that the chief vegetation of the cold continent that surrounds the South Pole consists of lichens and a few mosses and creeping liverworts. When we turn our attention to the North Polar regions we find more or less the same thing to be true, even though many flowering plants are present. Even here, however, the most abundant plants are lichens. Beyond the Arctic Circle there are 155 kinds of flowering and similar plants as compared to 413 kinds of lichens. In Greenland, alone, there are more than a hundred different lichens.

In Arctic regions lichens grow upon the ground, on other plants, and upon exposed rocks and cliffs. These latter lichens receive abundant supplies of nitrates from the droppings of the birds which stimulate a rich lichen growth. Near the seashores of Arctic islands, however, there are rarely many lichens; they cannot survive the winter ice storms. While lichens of various

This attractive lichen (Cladonia) is often called the "British soldier" lichen because of its bright red cap or head. Here it is growing among mosses at high altitude. It is closely related to reindeer moss.

kinds are characteristic plants of this frigid region, the reindeer mosses—which are lichens—are the most important since they furnish food for reindeer. In fact, the reindeer "pastures" of northern Scandinavia consist of ground-living lichens.

In our discussion of the lichen flora of Antarctica we raised the question of the ways in which these little plants could have become established. The same question arises in the case of Arctic lichens. The Arctic, too, was once warm and lichens have probably lived there for many millions of years. It is of interest that some kinds of lichens are found completely surrounding the North Polar region but are not found in warmer regions to the south. Yet these same cold-climate lichens occur also in Antarctica at the opposite end of the earth! How these lichens became established in both Antarctic and Arctic regions, but nowhere in between, is another botanical mystery. It is possible that far-flying birds may carry lichens to new areas. Some lichenologists, however, have suggested that perhaps high mountain ranges once connected the North and South Polar regions and that some lichens spread from one end of the earth to the other in this way. Even now, of course, a more or less continuous mountain range extends all the way from Alaska to the southern tip of South America. In any case, it is estimated that more than thirty kinds of lichens are found in both North and South Polar regions, but occur nowhere in between.

If you think it is unusual for lichens to be found growing in the frigid, unfriendly regions of the North and South Poles, then consider the fact that scientists believe that if life exists on other planets it may well be in the form of lichens or other leafless plants. These hardy little growths may one day prove to be existing in outer space. There is good reason to think so.

Of all the planets, it seems that Mars would be the one most likely to be inhabited by living things, either plant or animal. Nothing now known of the Martian environment rules out the possibility of life there. To support life as we know it, oxygen

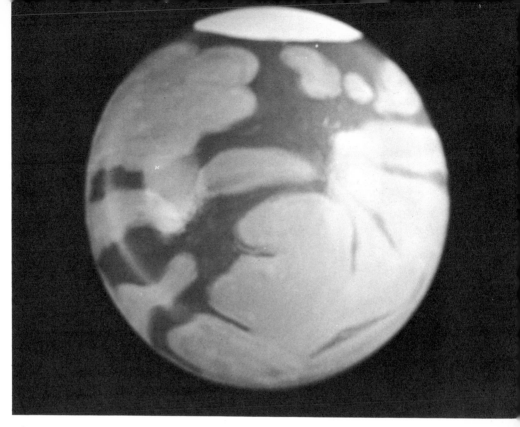

This is a model of the planet Mars, the red planet named for the Greek god of war. At the top is the white polar cap that shrinks and expands with the changing Martian seasons. Shown also are the so-called "canals," which may possibly be patches of vegetation.

must be present. The Martian atmosphere contains little free oxygen, but it does contain carbon dioxide, or oxygen in combination with carbon, and life of some form may be able to exist on this amount. Ultraviolet light from the sun penetrates the thin Martian atmosphere in heavy dosages, an amount that would probably kill earthly plants and animals. But life on Mars may have found a means of protection from these rays, or possibly a means of using this sun energy as its own source of energy.

There are several reasons for suspecting that vegetation of some sort is actually present on the surface of Mars. The white polar caps of the planet expand during the Martian winter and decrease in size as summer approaches. The reddish areas turn

If lichens occur on Mars then it is probable that fungi or fungus-like plants are also found there. It is possible that fungus spores might drift through space and germinate on other planets. Shown here are earth fungi which grow on decaying leaves.

dark from time to time, and reddish-brown areas take on a greenish-blue coloration. These changes suggest that some sort of seasonal growth of vegetation takes place, that there are seasonal changes on Mars as there are on earth.

The Martian climate is much colder than that on earth since it is farther from the sun. Still, Martian temperatures are within safe limits for lichens. It has been estimated that the noon temperature during the Martian summer reaches as high as 77°F. and that during the winter the temperature drops to as much as ninety degrees below zero. But you will recall that Antarctic lichens are able to live and grow upon rocks colder than this. We know they can survive such cold, especially when dry, and we know that Mars has a low humidity.

Much has been learned about Mars by means of spectrographic studies of the light reflected from its surface. Mariner

IV, the spacecraft that flew by Mars, recorded photographs of it, and future spacecraft will bring us more information and pictures from even closer range. Some day, in the not too distant future, space probes will land on the red planet. Then, perhaps, we will know for certain just what sort of biological life may exist there, if any.

If life is present, it is probably only some primitive form of plants such as the lichens that could live and flourish there. Some authorities doubt that it could be lichens because, they say, these plants grow too slowly and would not account for the rapid seasonal changes in color that seem to occur over the face of Mars. On the other hand, there may have evolved lichen-like plants of other types that grow more rapidly than do those we have on earth. Or life may have arisen independently on other planets. We are not saying that lichens of the types we know occur on Mars, but that of all the plants we know, only the lichens would seem most able to survive there.

Are there plants on other planets? We just do not know yet. Plans are underway for the extensive Martian research program that will be necessary before we have any definite answers. Should it be true that lichens or lichen-like plants are thriving on Mars, the story of the leafless plants will have a new and exciting chapter added to it.

This close-up of porous lava from the Craters of the Moon area shows how lichens creep over its surface. In time, these lichens will etch away the hard lava, creating soil where plants of other types can grow.

CHAPTER 7

The Uses of Lichens

To those of us who live in the United States, lichens have little practical value except as makers of soil. By the acids they secrete, rocks and sand are etched away and soil is created for higher forms of plant life. Like prison inmates, they work on rock piles, slowly reducing them to fine particles. As a visit to any cemetery will prove, they also quickly cover any exposed granite or marble surface and etch it away. Lichens of certain types also creep over the ground and form solid masses, especially in situations that are unfavorable to other forms of plant life. I know of a sandy field that for years remained barren of plant growth. Then, slowly, *Cladonia* lichens began creeping over the surface, followed by grasses and, later, by other plants. Before the lichens came there was only sand. The lichens were the pioneers.

While lichens do not attract much attention in our country at present, it is possible that they may do so in the future. This is because certain lichen fungi have been found to produce several highly colored compounds that inhibit or prevent the growth of bacteria. In this regard, you may recall that many of the new "wonder drugs" such as penicillin are derived from fungi of other types.

In other parts of the world, lichens have often been used in medicine but, unfortunately, most of these uses have little or no scientific basis. However, there is a lichen in Iceland that produces a mucilaginous substance that has useful properties as a laxative. Due to its special characteristics this material is also used in making puddings and as a sizing for paper and calico. It is also used for making bacterial culture media.

In former years our ancestors, of necessity, relied upon natural drugs and plant extracts for medicines. Some of these "cures" were useless. It was once believed that, in order to cure an ailment, a plant, or an extract from it, should be used that resembled the organ or part of the body afflicted. This was called the Doctrine of Signatures, For example, to prevent falling hair, a tonic was made from the threadlike strands of old-man's-beard lichen (*Usnea barbata*). This lichen is common in almost all parts of the world. Another lichen (*Lobaria pulmonaria*), a species that more or less resembles a lung, was used for lung troubles.

The use of lichens in medicine goes back many thousands of years. As long ago as 1600 B.C. a common lichen (*Evernia furfuracea*) was used in Egypt. Dry remains of these lichens were found in an ancient vase there. The people who lived along the Nile also used lichens to preserve the odor of spices in embalming mummies.

Color was sometimes considered to indicate a lichen's usefulness. A yellow lichen (*Xanthoria parietina*) was supposed to be good for jaundice, which turns a person's skin yellow. Another lichen, a kind that is covered with small wartlike spots, was used in curing rashes on children. The "dog lichen" (*Peltigera canina*) was believed to be helpful in curing hydrophobia. Of special interest, and most gruesome of all, was a lichen (*Parmelia saxatilis*) sometimes found growing on old human skulls and other bones. This was called "skull moss" or, in medical terminology, *muscus cranni humani*. It was supposed to cure epilepsy and sometimes sold for its weight in gold! The term *saxatilis* is of Latin origin and refers to its habit of growth on

98

Creatures of many kinds live and feed in the lichen "pastures" on trees and rocks. Here a slug, greatly enlarged, crawls among lichens on a tree.

rocks. As late as 1865, lichens of various kinds were still being sold in the drugstores in England. Lichens can still be purchased in drug markets in Cairo, where they are sold under the name of "Kheba."

Lichens of some kinds are used in brewing beer, while others find use in the making of cosmetics. Anyone who has had a course in chemistry knows that a common laboratory indicator of acidity or alkalinity is *litmus* paper which turns pink in acids and blue in alkalies. Litmus, the substance in the paper that changes color, is obtained from several lichens, including at least two creeping types found here in the United States. These are *Roccella tinctoria* which is common on rocks in southern California, and *Ochrolechia tartarea* which grows upon rocks and trees in almost all parts of the United States. Litmus is probably the most widely used lichen product in this country at present.

Lichens are fed upon by a number of small creatures, including insects, snails and slugs. There are also moths of several kinds whose larvae feed upon lichens. One of these is the lichen

This moth caterpillar feeds upon lichens and covers its body with a case constructed of lichens. It is thus well camouflaged from its enemies.

moth belonging to the family Amatidae. Its technical name is *Lycomorpha pholus* and it is a small, black, day-flying moth having the bases of its wings marked with yellow. Its larvae feed upon lichens that creep over rocky surfaces. There are also several other moths, related to clothes moths, whose larvae are *lichenivorous* (lichen-eaters). Some of these live in protective cases they construct of lichen fragments. This family of lichen moths is Lithosiidae, the so-called footman moths, named thus because many kinds are dressed in attractive but gaudy hues. One kind is the striped footman moth (*Hypoprepia miniata*) which has scarlet front wings marked with gray stripes. Its hind wings are yellow with gray margins. There are about fifty different kinds of footman moths, most of whose caterpillars live on lichens.

Thus, the lichen "pastures" that often cover rocks, soil, and trees are places where a number of small creatures live. In addition to those that actually feed upon the lichens, there are other small animals that capture and devour the lichen feeders. If you will sometime take the trouble to search the bark of a lichen-covered tree you are apt to see a bit of lichen that seems to be animated in a very mysterious manner. It creeps about, sometimes with jerky movements. When disturbed it remains still, but when all is quiet it moves on again. If you will carefully pick up one of these "galloping" lichens you will find that beneath it is hidden a small, bright-eyed insect with long, sharp jaws. These insects, which are related to lacewing flies or aphis-lions, feed upon aphids and other small insects that live among the lichens. They attach bits of lichens to their backs as a means of camouflage. Other kinds use the dried remains of past meals of small insects to camouflage themselves. Up and down the trunks of trees these small creatures go, hitching along in a characteristic manner, always seeking prey. Technically, these little insects are *Hemerobiids* but they are commonly known as trash-carriers, a most appropriate name.

My first experience with lichen-carriers was on a small island in a large, semi-tropical swamp. (I called this bit of dry land my Island of Adventure because of the many unusual plants and animals found there.) Once, on a visit to the island, I noticed

This moth is the adult of the lichen caterpillar. It does not eat lichens, but lays its eggs among them.

Shown here, greatly magnified, is a clump of "galloping" lichen. Beneath this clump is a small insect (Hemerobiid) that attaches bits of lichen to its back as a means of camouflage as it crawls over lichen-covered tree bark. (See next photograph)

If the bits of lichen attached to a Hemerobiid insect are removed, it will be seen that there are bristle-covered appendages around its body which help to hold its load of lichens. Just below this insect is an aphid on which it feeds.

a piece of lichen jerking itself about over the bark of a hornbeam tree. I thought at first that my eyes were deceiving me. Investigation showed, however, that it was a *Hemerobiid* that had cleverly covered itself with green lichens which certainly protected it from most sharp-eyed birds.

To animals that feed upon lichens, their chief food value lies in the lichen starch (*lichenin*) they contain. Starches, you may recall, are converted into sugars by the animal body. If we compare the sugar content of lichens with that of potatoes we find that some lichens contain about one-third as much. Some lichens thus have a rather high food value, but they may also contain bitter and astringent acids which must first be soaked out. Some animals cannot eat lichens because of this bitter substance. On the other hand, the digestive systems of some snails secrete a lichen-dissolving enzyme called *lichenase* that aids in their digestion.

While lichens, at present, have little use as human food in our own country, they have, in past ages and in other lands, often been eaten. Strangely, the American Eskimo never has made any use of lichens even though foods are often scarce in Arctic lands. The American Indians, on the other hand, made use of some lichens such as *Alectoria jubata,* a kind that grows suspended from trees or on soil. The tribes that lived along our Pacific Coast ate "rock tripe" at almost every meal. Even early French forest travelers, or "courreur de bois," ate this "tripe de rocke" when other foods were scarce. "Rock tripe" was a name applied to lichens which grew abundantly over the surfaces of rocks and which flourished especially in the humid climate. Lichens are admittedly a poor type of food, but they have sometimes served as emergency nourishment. As a matter of fact, the U. S. Air Force has listed lichens as possible survival foods for personnel stranded in Arctic regions and the Office of Intelligence of the U. S. Navy made the following recommendations in a booklet entitled "Survival on Land and Sea" (1944):

Among the edible lichens of the North are reindeer moss and Iceland moss which resembles it. These are low, mosslike plants with a network of branching stems instead of leaves. To be eaten they must first be soaked in water, then dried, ground into a powder, and again placed in water for several hours before being boiled. This will produce a sticky porridge-like mixture which, though somewhat insipid to taste, has considerable food value.

Another edible lichen that may be prepared in the same way is rock tripe, a black or brown leathery lichen that grows abundantly on rocks all through the Arctic. It has broad fronds, 1 to 3 inches in diameter, folded or crinkled at the edges and attached to the rock at the center. Rock tripe is commonly used in the North as an emergency food. Sir John Franklin, Richardson and other early Arctic explorers lived for weeks on it with hardly any other food.

It should, however, be emphasized that some lichens may cause illness so they should be eaten with caution. Probably the lichen most used as human food is Iceland moss (*Cetraria islandica*) which is gathered and sold in some northern countries. It is dried and powdered and prepared for consumption by boiling. When cool, this broth sets into a jelly. Milk is sometimes added. Powdered Iceland moss is often added to cereals and mashed potatoes.

It is believed by some that the manna mentioned in the Bible as having been eaten by the Israelites was actually a desert lichen (*Lecanora esculenta*). This lichen grows in the mountainous areas and is sometimes blown by high winds down into the lowlands. In 1891 there was a "fall" of this "manna" in Turkey. It is still eaten by desert tribes.

Ground-living lichens are common in Greenland, northern Scandinavia, Siberia, Alaska and northern Canada. Here, on these lichen ranges, live musk ox, caribou, and domesticated reindeer. American caribou and Old World reindeer have quite similar food habits. Wild caribou are continually on the move, a habit which allows the slow-growing lichens upon which they feed to grow again. In Lapland, the natives herd their reindeer from one part of the range to another to prevent destruction by overgrazing. The nomadic people of Lapland are almost completely dependent upon reindeer, as are other tribes along the Arctic Sea across to Siberia. In Lapland, lichens are divided into two types; the term "jaegel" refers to lichens that grow upon the ground like grass and upon which reindeer are fattened. Those that grow upon stones and trees are called "gadna" and are fed to reindeer only when the other type is not available.

Not only are Lapland reindeer pastured upon lichens, but lichens are harvested and stored much as we harvest and store hay for our livestock. After hand-harvesting, about ten years must pass before more lichens can be gathered from the same place. On the other hand, only about four years are needed for lichen pastures to regrow after grazing by reindeer. This slow growth is, of course, the reason why reindeer herds must continually be moved to new pastures. During especially severe winters, herds of Lapland reindeer often face starvation because they cannot feed upon the ice-covered lichens. During the winter of 1964-65, such conditions occurred in Lapland and an estimated 35,000 reindeer were saved by school children who collected mossy lichens and contributed them as forage. Ordinarily, the lichens collected by these children are sold in Germany where they are used as grave decorations.

Due to the rather low food value of lichens, a Lap farmer having ten cows and a few sheep must gather about sixty sledge loads of lichens for winter fodder. About five acres of land are needed to produce this much lichen food, and it must be remembered that a farmer can harvest the crop from this land only once in ten years. For this reason he must have a large acreage available.

The lichens or "reindeer mosses" most used for forage in the northern regions are *Cladonia rangiferina* and related kinds. What is most unusual about the distribution of this lichen is that it grows upon the ground all the way across northern United States and southward into Florida. Such wide distribution of a plant, all the way from Arctic regions to the tropics, is very rare. Other kinds of *Cladonias* are found growing upon the ground, on stones and rotten wood almost everywhere. In fact, they are probably our most common lichens. While the lichens mentioned above are the most common forage type in Arctic regions, several other kinds are found there that also furnish animal food.

In addition to their use as reindeer forage, Arctic lichens often serve as food for pigs. Young pigs seem to grow better on a mixture of reindeer moss and ordinary feed than upon the latter alone. In some sections of Scandinavia, reindeer moss is called *svinamose* (swine-moss).

Some lichens, in the past, have furnished dyes and certain chemicals used in industry. Many kinds contain oxalic acid used in the tanning of leather. Dyes obtained from lichens have been used for centuries. Now, of course, synthetic aniline dyes have replaced most of the old coloring materials. In ancient times, lichens of the family *Roccellaceae*, which are erect, branching types, were called Orchella mosses and much used as sources of dye. In fact, this dye was mentioned by such ancient writers as Theophrastus and Pliny, and it is also referred to in the Bible. These dyes were blue and red, and the lichens that produced them were known in industry as "weeds." This "weed" was imported into Europe from many foreign countries. As late as 1935, the last period for which figures are available, 411,265 pounds of lichen "weed" were imported into England. In France, a purple-blue dye was obtained from another kind of lichen. In other countries, also, lichens furnished dye materials. In northern Europe, brown and yellow colors were imparted to fabrics. Crocks of mashed lichen, called "crottle," were always kept in

Reindeer moss (Cladonia rangiferina) *has the widest range of any lichen. It occurs from beyond the Arctic Circle southward to Florida. In Britain, it is common on the high Scottish moors. It constitutes the chief forage of reindeer in Lapland and other northern countries.*

Scottish households for use in dying homespuns. Lungwort—a lichen—gave black color, while another lichen (*Roccella tinctoria*) was used to give British broadcloth an attractive blue color.

The dye-producing characteristics of lichens are due to the presence of lichen acids. These acids, it has been found, come from the fungus within the lichen and not from the green alga.

It is a far cry from a lichen growing on a rock or the trunk of a tree to a blooming flower, but it is a strange fact that lichens have been, and still are, used in the perfume industry. Mostly they are used to "hold" or "fix" the perfumes obtained from flowers. Various lichens, called oak-moss, are harvested in the Alps and other places and purchased by perfumers. This oak-moss is baled and exported to America and other countries.

Parmelia *lichens are common on tree bark where birds collect and use them in nest construction. Birds that commonly cover the outsides of their nests with lichens include the ruby-throated hummingbird, the blue-gray gnatcatcher, and the wood pewee.*

This ruby-throated hummingbird nest is covered with Par-melia lichens, perhaps as a means of camouflage.

Here, the essential oil, called extract of oak-moss, which consists mostly of *lichenol*, is used in the manufacture of scented soaps and other products. The thing about these lichen extracts that makes them of special value to the perfume industry is the fact that they harmonize or blend well with many flower essences and give them "freshness." Cyprus powder, a mixture of several kinds of powdered lichens, was once scented with other aromatic substances including musk, ambergris, oil of roses, jasmine, or orange blossom. Powdered lichen (*Ramalina calicaris*), which is white in color, was used to whiten the hair of wigs in place of starch.

While some lichens have bitter or sour tastes, most kinds are not poisonous. There are certain kinds, however, that may contain poisons. For example, one lichen (*Evernia vulpina*), when mixed with other substances, is supposed to be effective as a wolf poison. Another lichen that may be poisonous is a greenish-gray kind (*Cetraria juniperina*) that grows on rocks, trees, or old wood in the northern portions of the United States. This kind, also, has been used to poison wolves. In Wyoming it was recently discovered that lichens growing on soil containing large amounts of poisonous selenium contained enough of the material to affect sheep and cattle. It has also been found that cats are especially sensitive to lichen poisons.

It was mentioned previously that lichens are used in the brewing industry. In Russia and Siberia, they are used in place of hops, but the beer produced is said to be very bitter and highly intoxicating. In former years, large quantities of brandy were made from lichen alcohol in Sweden. This industry flourished until all the local lichens were harvested and used up. One pound of fermenting lichens produced about four ounces of alcohol.

Even though lichens are not as important in the modern world as in the past, they are still useful to the peoples who dwell in colder, northern regions.

109

Liverworts spread their green, leafy growths over rocks or soil in damp, shady places. What appear to be leaves are not true leaves because of their inner structure. This liverwort's botanical name is Conocephalum.

CHAPTER 8

Liverworts: The Creeping Plants

Liverworts are strange, creeping plants, usually leaflike in form, which grow in damp places. Favorite locations are moist cliffs and shady stream banks where mosses also grow. It seems quite appropriate that both liverworts and mosses should be found in similar situations since they have similar past histories. All these little plants have ancient lineages; they originated millions of years ago when climates were probably wet and tropical. During the millions of years they have lived on the earth the liverworts have likely changed but little; they got in an evolutionary rut and remained there while other plants slowly changed and eventually developed into modern trees and flowering plants. They are truly a backward group, of little importance as far as man is concerned. However, they are of special interest to biologists since they furnish important clues to the evolutionary history of plants. Aside from their scientific interest, they are a part of the world's flora and add attractive touches to the places where they grow.

You may not know liverworts as such, but it is probable that you have seen them. Perhaps you thought they were some sort of moss. In truth, they are not very closely related to the mosses at all but belong to a separate class of plants, the *Hepaticae,* a name which comes from the Greek word, *hepat,* meaning "liver." The common name, liverwort, refers to the shape of

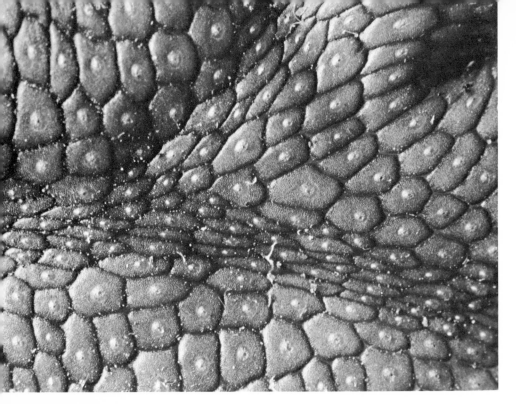

This close-up of a Conocephalum *"leaf" shows that its surface is marked off in more or less diamond-shaped areas. There is a* stomate *or breathing pore at the center of each one.*

some common kinds which resemble a lobed liver. As a result, they were once used as cures for liver ailments. *Wort* is an old English name meaning "plant."

While mosses usually bear leafy shoots that stand erect in clusters, the liverworts are usually flat and grow like branching ribbons over the ground. They anchor themselves down by means of tiny, rootlike *rhizoids.* Some liverworts are leafy but still they creep over the ground in more or less typical, liverwort fashion.

Like mosses, the liverworts have quite complicated life histories. A common kind found in most localities is *Marchantia.* This kind reproduces in two ways. If you will examine a group of growing *Marchantia* liverworts, especially in early spring, you will probably see a number of small, cuplike structures attached to their upper surfaces. Within these cups are minute, spherical bodies called *gemmae*. If one of these gemmae is carried or washed away to a new location it will grow into a new plant. This is a type of vegetative propagation somewhat similar to the way in which strawberry runners take root and grow and produce new plants. It should be understood that gemmae are in no way similar to seeds, since liverworts do not produce seeds.

Marchantia's other reproductive method is much more complex. There are two kinds of plants: male and female. In early spring, small, umbrella-shaped growths appear on the plants; those on the female plants have finger-like projections from their margins. Usually there are nine of these "fingers." The umbrellas on the male plants have small, disclike tops with scalloped edges. It is in these umbrellas that the male cells are produced. During rains, the male cells are splashed upon nearby female umbrellas in which egg cells are found and it is here that fertilization occurs. In time, spores are produced which are

A liverwort plant may be either male or female. Shown here are male sperm-producing heads. Sperm produced here swim or are splashed by rain to the female plants. The leafy shoots at the bottom are mosses which grew among the liverworts.

Here we see a spore head arising from a female plant. Spores produced within this head may give rise to other liverworts.

liberated and carried away by winds. These, if they alight upon suitable places, may grow into more liverworts. It is estimated that about 63 million spores are produced by each female umbrella. It is necessary that this large number be produced because of the small chance that any of them will fall in places suitable for growth.

Besides *Marchantia,* there are several other liverworts that grow in wet places. One of the most attractive of these is a large kind called *Conocephalum.* I have seen the entire surfaces of damp, rocky ledges near streams covered with the attractive mats of these plants in both the Ozark and Great Smoky Mountains. Other liverworts grow upon logs or the bark of living trees.

Closely related to the liverworts are the horned liverworts, *Anthoceros,* often found in similar places. These plants resemble

114

These plants are hornworts or horned liverworts. They grow in damp places as do the liverworts. Spores are produced in these stalks, which arise from the flat, creeping plant which resembles an ordinary liverwort.

Seen here are two spore-producing capsules of a hornwort (Anthoceros). *These capsules split lengthwise, liberating the spores.*

ordinary liverworts but, instead of producing umbrella-shaped growths for the production of spores, their spores are produced in slender, needle-like columns or capsules that arise from the surfaces of the creeping plants. Appropriately, these primitive plants are also known as hornworts.

There is one quite interesting thing about these plants that deserves special mention. On the lower surface of hornworts are many minute pores resembling stomates or breathing pores. Blue-green algae (*Nostoc*) often grow within these tiny chambers. Since these blue-green algae are able to "fix" nitrogen from the air and thus make it available for plant use, it seems probable that the hornwort may derive benefit from the algae that grow within its pores. Hornworts are able to grow without the algae but they grow better if the algae are present. This is another example of symbiosis, where two plants live together and both are benefited.

CHAPTER 9

The Mosses: Plants with a Past

*E*very plant has its "day in the sun," a time in world history when it plays an important role in the realm of living things. The heyday of the mosses lies far in the past; there was a time, about 300 million years ago, when giant moss plants of treelike form flourished in the dank, tropical forests. This was long before the coming of the flowering plants so familiar to us today and which add so much color to our lives. Thus, the ancient moss forests had no colorful blooms, but the bright greens and pastel shades of the mosses and other primitive plants were no doubt very beautiful. No human eyes were present to appreciate the strange beauty of this ancient world and all our knowledge about it has been obtained from the study of fossilized plant remains.

The mosses of the modern world are all small; they are merely survivors out of the world's dim past when their ancestors were larger and more important. Thus, mosses are of interest, not so much because of what they are but of what they once were. In a way, they are fugitives out of a world that no longer exists but, like other small leafless plants, they furnish botanists with important clues to the habits of ancient forms of plant life.

The name "moss" is quite confusing since many other plants including lichens, algae and Spanish moss are also called mosses. True mosses are classified as *Bryophytes,* a term derived from

117

Mosses creep over rocks and soil in shady, damp places. This Hypnum *moss has a rich luster like the most expensive carpet.*

two Greek words, *bryon* meaning "moss" and *phyton* meaning "plant." Botanists are not in complete agreement as to the past history of these little plants; some believe that they form a link between the water-living algae and the land-inhabiting ferns, while other botanists believe that the ferns were evolved directly from the algae and that the mosses were not a link in the chain. In any case, the moss tribe is very old and arose during the time when modern plants were just beginning to evolve.

In the summer of 1833 there occurred a great volcanic eruption on the island of Krakatoa near Java. During the eruption, all life on the island was destroyed, leaving nothing but hot, barren lava. In time, the lava cooled and airborne spores of algae were carried to the island by winds. These germinated, producing green algal growths over the rocks. Soon the algae were followed by mosses whose spores also came by winds. The mosses anchored themselves in the lava and etched away the surface, creating minute quantities of soil where the seeds of flowering plants eventually found suitable sites for growth. What happened on Krakatoa is a classic example of the way in which mosses and other spore-producing plants become established on cooled volcanic rocks.

But you do not need to travel to far-off Krakatoa to see how mosses grow on cooled lava beds. If you visit the Craters of the Moon in Idaho you will see a vast area covered by an ancient

Mosses can survive under very adverse conditions. This clump of moss grew on the barren lava beds of Craters of the Moon in Idaho.

Dense growths of Polytrichum *moss plants remind one of an airplane view of a dense pine forest. These plants are about an inch tall.*

lava flow that spreads over many square miles. It is a strange region of black, twisted stone and deep crevasses where travel by foot is very difficult. Vegetation is scant, consisting of small shrubs and trees that survive in the small pockets of soil. Here also, in spring, grow pretty mariposa lilies, their gay colors in startling contrast to the barren landscape. But what impresses one most is the fact that the black, pitted lava is covered with lichens and small, cushion-like growths of mosses. The mosses and lichens turn green and begin growth again each spring when rains sweep over the dreary landscape, but when the black lava beds become heated by the summer sun, they cease growth and become dormant, awaiting the return of life-giving moisture. In the ancient days, soon after this lava had cooled, it is probable that lichens and mosses were the first plants to establish themselves, just as they did on the island of Krakatoa.

While mosses are very common in almost all localities, they are not very conspicuous since they are small and tend to grow in hidden, damp places. In the world there are about 23,000 different kinds. In size, present-day mosses range from a sixteenth of an inch to nearly two feet, but most kinds are little more than two inches tall. While a moss plant consists of a green, leafy stem, what appear to be leaves are not true leaves, nor are the rootlike structures at the base of the moss plant true roots even though they serve more or less the same purpose. The stems of moss plants do not have efficient water tubes or conductive systems as do most larger plants. This may perhaps be the reason why they do not grow to large size.

A moss plant begins life as a microscopic spore that germinates on damp soil, on rocks, tree bark, or fallen logs. Here, the

Greatly enlarged moss spores. If these should fall on suitable places they will germinate and produce green moss plants.

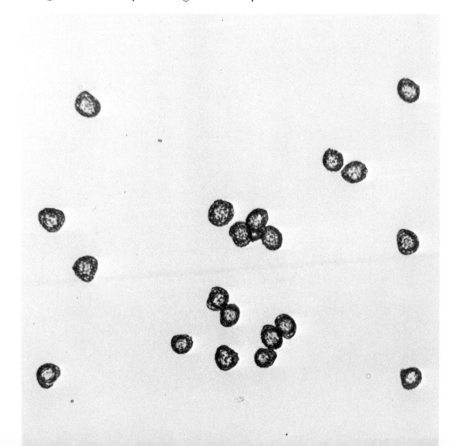

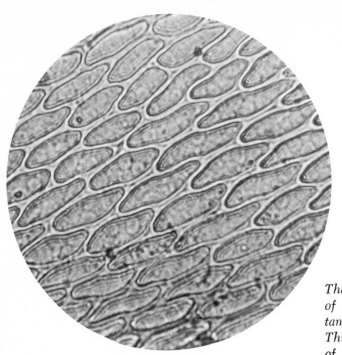

The microscopic structure of moss "leaves" is important in their identification. This is a photomicrograph of a moss "leaf" (Semato- phyllum) showing the characteristic shape of the cells.

This photomicrograph of a moss (Chamberlainia) shows the cells of its "leaves." Compare this with the photograph above.

This close-up of Mnium *moss reveals the details of its green "leaves."*

spore absorbs moisture and a slender thread or filament grows out. This filament eventually divides into branches, some of which lose their green chlorophyll and enter the ground where they serve as roots or rhizoids. Upright shoots also arise along which develop green "leaves." This part of the moss plant's life cycle is called the *gametophyte* or sexual state and, in time, male or female "flowers" or leafy rosettes develop at the tip of each moss plant. Sometimes both sexes are located on the same plant and in other cases they are on separate plants. In spring, these

Close-up of "flowers" of Mnium *moss plants. The reproductive organs can be seen at the center of each one. Sometimes the "petals" of moss "flowers" are colored like those of true flowers. In some mosses, both male and female organs are in the same "flower," while in others they are separate. After fertilization, a slender spore stalk grows up out of the "flower."*

flower-like rosettes are formed at the tip of each plant and it is within these "flowers" that the sex cells are located. During periods of heavy dew or rain the male cells swim to the female cells where fertilization occurs. In the case of a flowering plant, the fertilized egg cells develop into seeds, but in the case of the moss plant the fertilized egg cell develops into a slender stalk which grows up from the "flower" and which is usually brown or yellowish in color. At the tip of this stalk is an enlarged spore capsule covered by a tiny, hoodlike cap. This constitutes the *sporophyte* or spore-producing stage of the moss plant's life cycle.

When mature, the cap covering the spore capsule is shed, exposing an opening around which is a ring of "teeth." Generally these teeth are sensitive to moisture and bend outward during dry weather so that the contained spores may sift out and be carried away by winds. During damp weather the teeth bend inward, closing the spore capsule. There is an interesting thing about these teeth: depending upon the kind of moss, there are always the same number of teeth—four, sixteen, thirty-two, or sixty-four. The number of teeth is related to the basic genetics of the plants. In the case of *Sphagnum* moss, when the cap covering the spore capsule dries out and compresses the air within it, considerable pressure develops. Eventually, this pressure causes the cap to pop off, throwing the spores for some distance. These little "explosions" sound like corn popping, though not as loud.

Here are seen the stalked spore capsules or sporophytes *of urn moss* (Physcomitrium). *Eventually, the caps will be shed, liberating the spores.*

Spore capsules of mosses are of many shapes. The ones seen here are Ptychomitrium, *a rather rare moss in most places.*

Like the heads of graceful swans, these hooded spore capsules of Funaria *nod on their stalks.*

When the hoods or caps of the spore cases are shed, it can be seen that there are teeth surrounding the capsule opening. During dry weather these teeth spread apart, releasing the spores.

This, in brief, is the life story of a moss plant from spore to spore. Being primitive plants, they do not produce seeds with hard coats which may remain alive a long while even though they dry out. It is probable that the life histories of the ancient mosses were very similar to those of the present day. Time, in its passing, has had but little effect on the basic life stories of these lowly little plants. Thus do today's mosses give us clues to the ways of the ancient plants.

127

As a biologist, I am often asked, "What good is this moss or this insect?" People always seem to regard all other animals, as well as plants, as things which have been placed upon the earth for their own special enjoyment or economic use. The moss (or insect) might equally ask, "What good is man?" We all—the plants, the insects, and the other creatures—exist in the world together. No plant or animal was evolved for the special benefit of another. From the human standpoint, mosses are not of much economic importance; we do not "use" them for anything much. Yet, they do add touches of beauty to forests and rocky glens and they actually do have some economic value.

Probably the chief thing that gives mosses, especially *Sphagnum* moss, their economic importance is their amazing ability to absorb and hold large quantities of water. A moss plant is made up of two kinds of cells. One kind is very large and has thin walls with circular openings leading from one to the other. Among these cells are other, smaller, cells filled with colorless jelly and granules of green chlorophyll. When water falls upon a moss plant it is quickly absorbed into the large cells through the openings in their walls and then on into the adjoining cells. Soon all the cells are full of water. This is the plant's method of storing water. Gradually, this water is absorbed into the small cells and used by the green chlorophyll in food manufacture. As in all green plants, mosses use the energy of the sun in making starch and sugar from water and from carbon dioxide obtained from the air. When weather is dry the water-storage cells become empty and the moss plant loses its vivid green coloration and curls up. When dry, some mosses turn almost white. When rains come again, water is quickly absorbed and the plant starts its growth processes once more. Few other plants have such amazing abilities to lie dormant during long periods of drought and then begin life again when rains fall.

It is this ability of mosses to absorb and store large quantities of water that makes them ideal for use by florists and nurseries

128

Hair-cap mosses (Polytrichum) *are common in most places. The hoods of their spore capsules are hairy.*

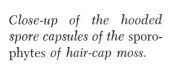

Close-up of the hooded spore capsules of the sporophytes of hair-cap moss.

in packing plants for storage and shipment. A small quantity of *Sphagnum* moss, for example, will hold many times its own weight of water. For this reason it also makes an ideal material for surgical dressings. As compared to cotton, which will absorb only five or six times its weight of water, *Sphagnum* moss will absorb and hold nearly twenty times its own weight. It also retains water better than cotton due to the fact that the water is absorbed into its cells. This same characteristic has enabled it to grow in places where no other plant could survive because of infrequent rains. In some northern countries, including Canada, northern Europe, Scandinavia and the British Isles, *Sphagnum* or peat moss has been growing for thousands of years and the remains of these plants have gradually accumulated to considerable depths in the form of peat. This peat, when dry, is an excellent fuel. In Ireland and Scotland, for example, peat has been the chief fuel for centuries. In fact, it was once the only fuel supply available to the peasantry. While peat will hold up to 200 times its weight of water, when cut into blocks and dried it makes an excellent fuel that burns very well. For heating purposes, it is about half as efficient as good coal but gives off twice as much heat as wood. It also gives off but little smoke. Reclaimed peat bogs are always very fertile. It is estimated that one-fifth of the most fertile land in England and Ireland was once peat bog. In northern United States, there are probably about 12 million tons of peat that could be used for fuel. The formation of peat beds is actually the first step in the creation of coal.

The formation of peat bogs in northern areas has been studied in considerable detail. Peat bogs begin as shallow lakes or ponds. *Sphagnum* moss begins growing around the margins and, gradually, pushing outward. The dead moss sinks to the bottom and slowly turns into peat. Over the top of this accumulating peat, more *Sphagnum* grows, always growing out from the shore. Little by little the area of open water becomes smaller

Sphagnum *moss grows in many localities, but it is especially abundant in cooler parts of the country where it often forms large mats on bogs. In time, these turn into peat beds.*

and smaller as the lake fills up with peat. Eventually, nothing remains but a spongy peat bog. Cranberry bogs were also formed in this way.

It is a strange fact that *Sphagnum* mosses not only form peat bogs on level land but also form "climbing" bogs that extend up slopes away from water. This is possible because of the tremendous water-conducting ability of the moss. Water is absorbed from a pond or stream and passes from plant to plant up the slope. In Europe, such bogs often climb as high as twenty feet above the level of the lake from which they obtain their water supply.

Peat bogs are not only interesting because of their manner of formation, but they can be dangerous as well. People as well as animals are often trapped in these soft "quaking bogs" just as in quicksand. In Ireland, it was once believed that evil spirits inhabited the remote peat bogs and the fact that eerie, dancing lights were often seen in such places added to the belief. The fact that people often disappeared in these bogs was ascribed to the evil spirits believed to dwell there. Actually, the mysterious lights seen floating over the bogs were will-o'-the-wisps or masses of burning *methane* gas given off by the decaying vegetation. The people who disappeared had, of course, been trapped by the treacherous bog and sank out of sight.

Due to some substance contained in *Sphagnum* moss, or in the peat into which it turns, animals or plants that sink into peat bogs are often well preserved for long periods. Viking ships of wood, for example, have been found in such bogs where they have been preserved for many centuries. Peat bogs are usually of a uniform temperature all year. As a result, butter was often buried in Irish peat bogs as a means of refrigeration. Sometimes, when these old caches are found, the butter is still in good condition even after long periods of storage.

Recently, some very interesting discoveries of ancient weapons of war have been found at four locations on the island of Fünen in Denmark. These objects were well preserved in the peat beds by the high concentrations of tannic acid occurring there. Among the weapons found were swords, lances, spears, axes, bows, arrows, shields, chain mail, helmets, scabbards and other articles of ancient wars such as buckles, knives, flints, wagon parts, and pottery. Most of the weapons were of the type used by the Germanic tribes against the Roman invaders during the fourth and fifth centuries. Some of the weapons were of Roman origin, suggesting that they were the spoils of war or perhaps had been obtained by barter with the enemy.

Why had these war implements been dumped in these places? This is a question that has been answered in part by a study of ancient writings. The places where the weapons and other war objects were located were once open lakes that had gradually

Sphagnum *moss has great water-absorbing capacity. Here a handful of wet moss is being squeezed. Note the streams of water flowing out of it.*

filled up with peat. In ancient times, it was often the custom to dump the weapons of defeated enemies into lakes as offerings to the gods of war. In other countries, victorious armies also, sometimes, dumped their own weapons into lakes as offerings. All such weapons, before being placed in such places, were always broken or bent so as to render them useless. All the war implements found preserved in the Danish peat beds had been made useless in various ways. Swords had been bent, and spears, shields and other weapons had been broken. This fact lends support to the idea that the weapons found preserved in the peat beds were actually offerings to the ancient gods. Due to the preservative action of the peat, the remains of horses, also, were preserved in these same beds. Evidently, horses, too, were considered to be military equipment since their remains indicate that they had been killed before being placed in the lake. Thus, *Sphagnum* moss, by its strange preservative characteristic, has been a boon to archaeologists, the scientists who delve into the histories of ancient peoples and their customs.

Mosses of various kinds have often been used as surgical dressing because of their ability to absorb moisture, but it has only recently been discovered that some mosses contain substances that inhibit, or slow down, the growth of bacteria and fungi. Of a number of mosses tested, three kinds were found to contain such substances. The first of these is *Anomodon postratus,* a common moss often found growing in damp places, especially at the bases of trees or on wet rocks. It occurs in the eastern half of the United States. The second moss is a western type named *Orthotrichum rupestre* that is often found on trees. The third kind, *Mnium cuspidatum,* is sometimes known as the "woodsy Mnium." It grows on soil in moist, shady places in woods or fields. This is a field of research that holds great possibilities for the discovery of important new antibiotic drugs. Only a few of the thousands of different kinds of mosses have, so far, been investigated.

Of special interest are the so-called copper mosses that grow abundantly in places where copper ores are found. These mosses are apparently able to use hydrogen sulfide gas instead of oxygen in their growth processes. They are very ancient mosses that probably arose when there was less oxygen in the air than at present. This fact proves that plant life may perhaps exist in the absence of abundant oxygen, a condition that prevails on some other planets such as Mars. Apparently these copper mosses obtain hydrogen sulfide gas from copper-sulfur compounds in cop-

134

per ore; thus their growth is considered to be a reliable clue to the presence of copper. Some mosses show preference for either acid or alkaline soils and may, thus, serve as reliable indicators of such soil conditions.

Another interesting moss is luminous moss, *Schistostega*, a kind often found growing in caves, dark holes in the ground, or under the roots of trees. It has also been known to grow in abandoned cellars. This strange little moss has its cells shaped like tiny lenses that catch the light rays in dimly lighted places and focus them on the green chlorophyll granules located at the bottoms of the cells. This enables the plant to manufacture food, even in feeble light. Luminous moss is rather rare and its discovery by a moss student is a noteworthy event. In the dim light of the places where it grows it seems to emit a golden-greenish light like the eyes of a cat. The truth, of course, is that it gives off no light of its own, but merely collects and reflects the small amount of daylight that enters the dimly lighted places where it grows. Certainly, it is one of nature's curiosities.

Let us next consider the club mosses, which are not really true mosses but which are included here for convenience. Club mosses are classified as *Lycopodiums*, a group of plants that arose about 300 million years ago during the Paleozoic Era. The name, *Lycopodium*, is derived from two Greek words, *lyco* meaning "wolf" and *podium* meaning "foot." Just why these plants were given this name is unknown.

Along with the giant horsetails, the ancient club mosses were a conspicuous feature of prehistoric forests. These ancestors of the club mosses often grew to enormous size. Two kinds, *Lepidodendron* and *Sigillaria*, are well known from their fossilized remains. The name, *Lepidodendron*, comes from two Greek words, *lepido* meaning "scale" and *dendron* meaning "tree." The name refers to the scalelike surface markings on the trunks caused by the shedding of leaves. They are often called "scale trees." The name, *Sigillaria*, is from a Latin word, *sigillum*,

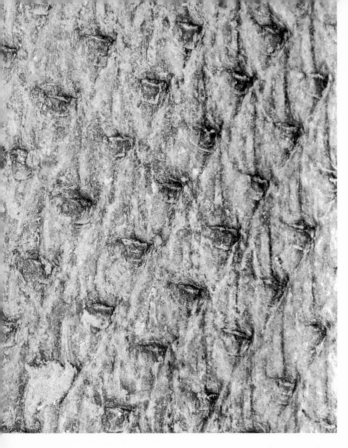

This close-up of a fossil scale tree or Lepidodendron *shows the scars where its "leaves" broke away. These large tree-mosses flourished many millions of years ago.*

meaning "seal." Thus, these latter, palmlike trees are known as "seal trees." The treelike club mosses often grew more than a hundred feet tall and at least three feet in diameter. Some kinds bore spore cones a foot long at the ends of their branches. But these remote ancestors of the club mosses are all extinct; they disappeared along the trail of time and only their small descendants remain in the modern world.

Modern club mosses are but a few inches tall. Unlike the true mosses, they have water-conducting tubes in their stems. This conducting system consists of two types as in ordinary trees or flowering plants; that is, there is a *xylem* or woody zone which carries water up the stem and a *phloem* zone which carries manufactured foods back down the stem from the leaves. In the case of the club mosses, however, these zones alternate with each other in both stems and roots, an arrangement which is unique among plants.

The yellowish spores of club mosses are often produced in great numbers and were once an item of commerce. They were used as coatings for pills and also in making fireworks since they burn with a flash explosion. In the early days of photography, lycopodium powder was used in taking flash pictures. Later, magnesium powder replaced this lycopodium powder. These spores were also used in medicine as a soothing powder for chafes and wounds. Because of their uniform size, they were also used as standards of microscopic measurement. Infusions of club moss plants contain substances that, in the past, made them useful as emetics and even as poisons.

In general, the life histories of club mosses are similar to those of true mosses but, due to the small size of the *gametophyte* stage, it is almost impossible to find. It lives in the soil and requires more than seven years to develop. Another ten years or so must pass before the young plant extends above the soil surface. Thus, about twenty years may be required for the full life

Ground pines or club mosses are related to true mosses. They creep along the ground in shady places, especially in deep forests.

Club mosses reproduce by means of spores as do true mosses. Spores are produced in cases located at the bases of the "leaves."

cycle to be completed from spore to spore. This is sufficient to discourage most biologists from growing club mosses from spores!

Due to the fact that most club mosses look somewhat like slender pine or spruce twigs that run along just above the surface of the ground, they are often called "running pines." Other names are applied to various kinds, including running cedar, ground cedar, foxtail club moss and shining club moss. There are about a hundred different kinds in the world. In the United States there are eleven kinds. Most of those that grow in the tropics live as *epiphytes;* that is, they live on the sides and limbs of growing trees as do air-plants such as Spanish "moss."

CHAPTER 10

Horsetails: The Living Fossils

To appreciate the horsetails we must consider their past history. We may appreciate a rose for itself because of its beauty and because it is a thing of the present, but to appreciate and understand a horsetail—or a moss—we must remember that most of its story lies in the past. The horsetails that live in modern times are merely fugitives or survivors out of a world and a time that no longer exist. They, like the mosses and related plants, had their heyday during Paleozoic time which was about 350 million years ago. It cannot be said that the appearance of the horsetails in the ancient world was one of Nature's errors any more than a pine tree or an oak is an error in modern times. The great horsetails lived and flourished for millions of years but, for some unknown reason, by the end of the Paleozoic, most of the treelike horsetails had passed away, leaving only their small descendants as living plants. Why the ancient horsetails disappeared is one of botany's unsolved riddles, which, like the passing of the giant dinosaurs, is a mystery that may never be solved.

While modern horsetails are of little economic importance, we owe them a debt since it was these plants and their relatives whose remains formed the coal beds which, for hundreds of years, have furnished us with our best fuel. The sun, shining down upon the ancient forests of giant horsetails and other plants, furnished the heat energy for the manufacture of the carbon compounds in their tissues. In effect, this ancient heat was stored in the coal, so the heat we feel from burning coal is "bottled" sunshine from the far-off days when the earth was young. It is our heritage from the plants of the past. Authorities estimate that there are more than 7,400 billion tons of coal in the world. These deposits are sometimes a mile in depth. Nearly half of this is in the United States; the rest is located in various other countries. If we continue to use coal at the present rate, the supply will probably last for about 3,000 years. Coal, as we have said, is formed by the accumulation of dead plant material, but it is estimated that a seam of coal a foot thick is the result of an original layer of vegetation about ten feet thick that was slowly compressed and changed. Thus, it is obvious that tremendous quantities of vegetation have lived and died during the earth's history to account for the amount of coal that was formed.

There were originally two types of horsetails; one type were the *Equisetums* and others were the *Calamites*. The name, *Equisetum*, is a Latin term meaning "horsetail," while *Calamites* comes from a Greek word, *Kalamites*, meaning "reedlike." The *Calamites* were giant, treelike horsetails with jointed stems and needle-like or lance-shaped leaves. They grew as tall as a hundred feet and were sometimes five feet across at their bases. They bore large cones or *strobili* within which were produced numerous spores. They had no seeds. The *Calamites* have long since passed into oblivion and we know them only from fossils. On the other hand, the *Equisetums* still grow in the modern world, though they are greatly reduced in size. Their remote ancestors, like the *Calamites*, were treelike. Why one type disappeared and the other survived we do not know. Evidently, something about their growth habits or way of life made it impossible for them to survive in the changing climates of the world, so they passed away. If you would like to see what these

Spore-producing horsetail shoots have spore cones or strobili. The stems are jointed and arise from underground stems or rhizomes.

Horsetails or Equisetums grow in many places, especially near woodland streams. Ancient horsetails grew to tree size. These present-day shoots are only a foot or two high.

This close-up of a mature horsetail cone or stro-bilus shows its details. Spores are produced in the white toothlike, or saclike, appendages.

ancient forests looked like you may do so by visiting one of the large natural history museums of the United States. Here you will find portions of such forests, beautifully and accurately reconstructed in great detail. These scenes are based on careful studies of fossil plants.

While ancient horsetails were very large, all modern kinds are quite small, although there is one vinelike horsetail found in South America that reaches a length of 36 feet. Most other kinds or species, of which there are twenty-five in the world, seldom grow more than a yard tall. Here in the United States there are about a dozen kinds, all small.

Equisetums grow in damp and, sometimes, shady places. Beneath the soil there is a horizontal, branched stem or rhizome. The upright stems grow up from these underground rhizomes. In some cases, tubers are produced on the rhizomes which serve as food-storage sites. In many kinds there are two types of upright stems. One type of stem is unbranched and bears a spore-bearing cone or *strobilus* (plural; strobili) at its tip; the other kind of stem is green and bushy with needle-like branches arranged in a circle around each joint or node. It is from this form of growth that the plant gets its name. Horsetail stems are hollow and very rough in texture. In a way, they resemble small bamboo plants because of their jointed stems. Since they contain

A close-up of an Equisetum *stem shows details of a joint. Note the rough texture of the stem which once made the plants useful as scouring agents.*

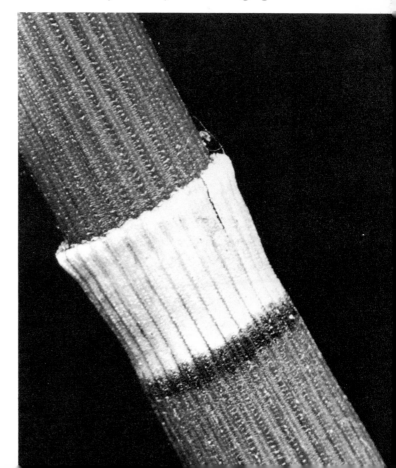

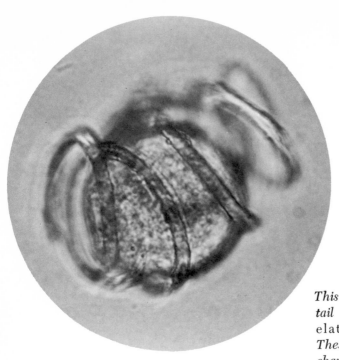

This greatly enlarged horse-tail spore shows its coiled elators or appendages. These coil and uncoil with changes in humidity and thus aid in dispersal of spores.

silica, the chief constituent of sand, they are very rough. If you rub your fingers over the stem it feels like sandpaper. Because of this rough texture they were often used by early settlers for scouring pots, pans, and floors. This, of course, was before the availability of the various scouring powders so much in use today.

In general, horsetails reproduce like mosses, but their spores are quite interesting. Each microscopic spore has four spoonlike spiral bands called *elators*. These are wound around the spore in a spiral. When dried out, these elators unwind and act like parachutes, enabling winds to pick them up and carry them for some distance.

While horsetails have little or no economic importance, they are an interesting feature of the world's vegetation and help us to understand the growth and reproductive habits of the plants of the long ago.

List of Manuals

FOR FURTHER STUDY OF LEAFLESS PLANTS

For those amateur botanists who wish to learn more about the plants discussed in this book, the following publications are recommended:

ALGAE

The Fresh-water Algae of the United States, by G. M. Smith. Published by McGraw-Hill, New York. Covers identification of fresh-water algae. Has many helpful drawings. (1950)

Marine Algae of the Northeastern Coast of Northern America, by W. R. Taylor. Published by University of Michigan Press, Ann Arbor. Covers identification of many marine algae. (1957)

FUNGI

Common Fleshy Fungi, by Clyde M. Christensen. Published by Burgess Publishing Company, Minneapolis. A ring-bound manual of mushrooms and other fungi, containing 237 pages and 200 black and white photographs. (1965)

Field Book of Common Mushrooms, by William S. Thomas. Published by G. P. Putnam's Sons, New York. This manual contains 367 pages with many color plates and black and white photographs. (1948)

Illustrated Genera of Wood Decay Fungi, by Charles L. Fergus. Published by Burgess Publishing Company, Minneapolis. This is a ring-bound manual containing 132 pages and many black and white photographs. While this is a technical manual, it is very helpful to the amateur. (1963)

Marvels of Mycetozoa, by W. Crowder. National Geographic Magazine, Vol. 49, 1926, pages 421-443. This is an excellent article, containing 16 color plates of common slime-molds.

The Lichen Flora of the United States, by Bruce Fink. Published by University of Michigan Press, Ann Arbor. Over 400 pages, 47 plates. This is a technical manual, but very helpful to the amateur. (1961)

The Observer's Book of Lichens, by K. A. Kershaw and K. L. Alvin. Published by Frederick Warne & Company, Inc., New York. Even though this is a British publication, it is helpful to American students of lichens since these plants are more or less worldwide in distribution. This little manual contains 126 pages, including 64 plates, some in color. (1963)

How to Know the Mosses and Liverworts, by Henry S. Conard. Published by Wm. C. Brown, Dubuque, Iowa. A ringbound manual containing 226 pages and numerous drawings and keys. Very helpful to the amateur. (1956)

Mosses with a Hand-lens, by A. J. Grout. Published by the author, Newfane, Vermont. This is an excellent manual with many drawings and a few photographs. (1947)

A Field Guide of the Ferns, by Boughton Cobb. Published by

Houghton Mifflin Company, Boston. While this manual is devoted mostly to the identification of ferns, it also contains sections on both horsetails *(Equisetums)* and club mosses *(Lycopodiums).*

The Fern Guide, by Edgar T. Wherry. Published by Doubleday & Company, Garden City, New York. Like the reference listed above, this manual is devoted mostly to ferns, but has keys and illustrations that are helpful in the identification of horsetails and club mosses. (1961)

Index

Page numbers in **boldface** are those on which illustrations appear.

149

151

The Author

Entomologist Ross E. Hutchins is also an expert nature photographer, and this combination of interests has resulted in almost thirty years of studying, photographing and writing about insects, plants, animals and birds. Born in Montana, he grew up on a cattle ranch near Yellowstone Park. At Montana State College he majored in biological sciences and later he received his Ph.D. in zoology and entomology from Iowa State College.

Dr. Hutchins' articles and pictures of natural history subjects have appeared in encyclopedias, books and magazines, among them *National Geographic, Life* and *Natural History*, as well as such European publications as *Sie und Er, La Vie des Bêtes* and *Sciences et Avenir*. His books in the juvenile field include CADDIS INSECTS, THE AMAZING SEEDS, and the companion volumes, THIS IS A LEAF, THIS IS A FLOWER, and THIS IS A TREE. All are noted for their remarkable close-up photographs by the author.

Ross Hutchins lives in Mississippi where he is Director of the State Plant Board of Mississippi and Professor of Entomology at Mississippi State University.

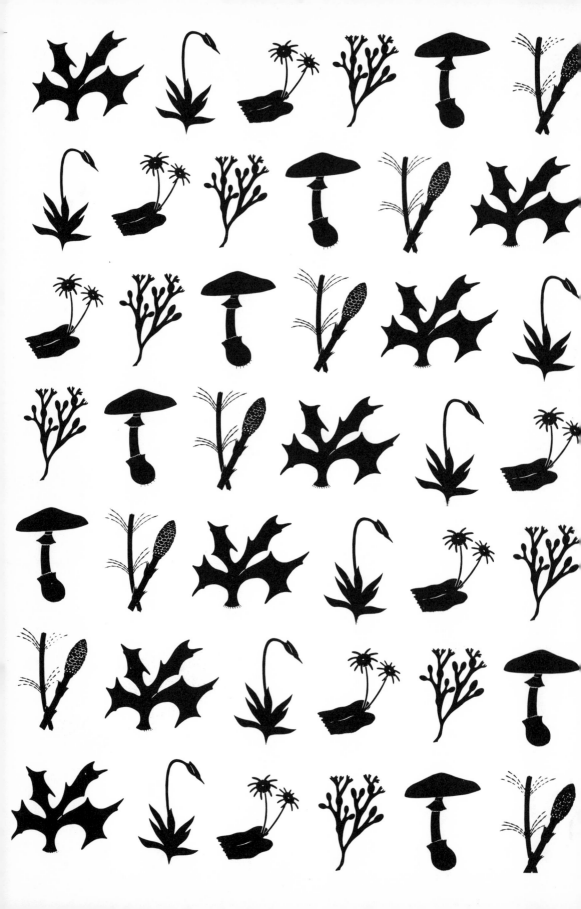

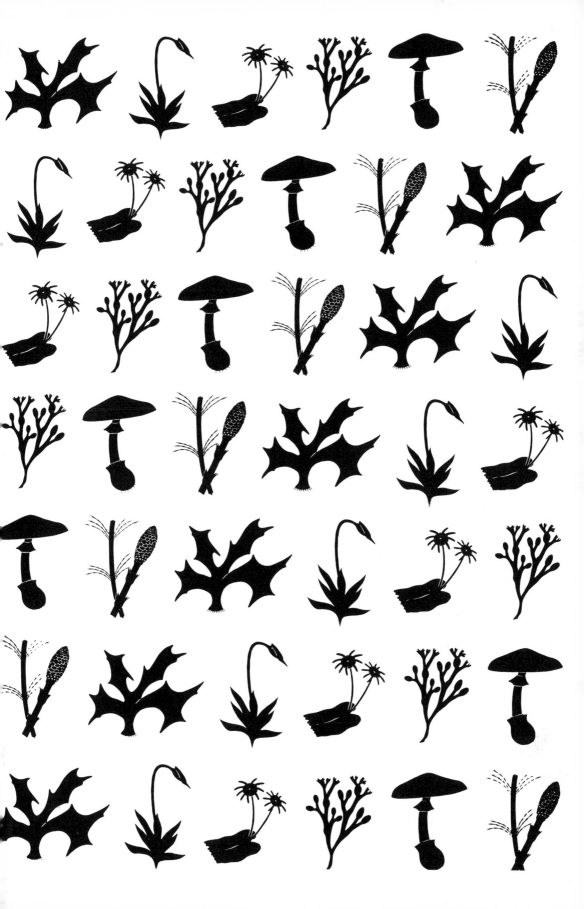